398.2 Garden, Nancy
G
    Vampires

VAMPIRES

VAMPIRES

NANCY GARDEN

J. B. LIPPINCOTT COMPANY
Philadelphia and New York

U.S. Library of Congress Cataloging in Publication Data

Garden, Nancy.
  Vampires.

  (The Weird and horrible library)
  SUMMARY: Examines the history and legends of the "undead" creatures
who have reportedly roamed the earth since ancient times, sucking the blood
of the living.
  Bibliography: p.
  1. Vampires—Juvenile literature. [1. Vampires] I. Title.
GR830.V3G37   398.2′1   72–13830
ISBN–0–397–31456–6   ISBN–0–397–31457–4 (pbk.)

To the feline Count Dracula

and my own witchcat

Timothy Pyewacket

ACKNOWLEDGMENTS

Pictures appearing on pages 19, 22, 29, 73, 98, 106, 116, 117, and 119, courtesy of the New York Public Library Picture Collection; pages 88, 89, 90, and 91, from *A Biography of Dracula* by Harry Ludlam with permission of the publishers, W. Foulsham and Co., Limited; pages 38 and 94, from *Dracula* (Universal, 1931), courtesy of Culver Pictures, Inc.; page 60, published by permission of University Books, Inc., Secaucus, New Jersey; page 46, courtesy Collection, The Museum of Modern Art, New York, The William B. and Evelyn A. Jaffe Collection; page 41, from *El Vampiro* (Abel Salazar/Cinematográfica A.B.S.A., 1959); pages 53, 65, and 69, from *The Horror of Dracula* (Hammer, 1958); pages 63 and 111, from *Dracula, Prince of Darkness* (Hammer, 1962); page 26, copyright © 1971 by Dan Curtis Productions, Inc.; page 81, from *In Search of Dracula* by McNally and Florescu (New York Graphic Society, Ltd.); page 83, from *In Search of Dracula* by McNally and Florescu (New York Graphic Society, Ltd.), permission Kunstmuseum, Vienna; page 85, courtesy Theater Collection, Lincoln Center Library of the Performing Arts.

7

ACKNOWLEDGMENTS

For much of the material in Chapter VII I am indebted to *A Biography of Dracula: The Life Story of Bram Stoker*, by Harry Ludlam, published for the Fireside Press by W. Foulsham and Co. Ltd., London, 1962.

For the material about the real Count Dracula, I am indebted to an article in the *Boston Globe* (Nov. 21, 1971) by Bill Fripp, called "Will the Real Count Dracula Stand Up?" in which Fripp reports on the researches of two Boston College professors, Raymond McNally and Radu Florescu, the latter of whom is distantly descended from the original Count.

CONTENTS

INTRODUCTION

It wasn't a particularly dark night, or a particularly spooky one either. Still, I was nervous, for no one was supposed to be in the musty old kitchen at that hour. My hunger was stronger than my fear or my respect for rules, however, and I was determined to find something to eat before I allowed myself to go back to my warm, friendly bed.

I wasn't at home, you see. I was at a summer stock theater, working for a producer who was so stingy he gave his large company of stagehands, actors, and technicians only the skimpiest of meals. He was smart to declare the kitchen off limits. We were all so perpetually hungry we would have eaten his pantry bare in a matter of minutes if given half a chance.

Because I wasn't supposed to be in the kitchen, I couldn't very well turn on a light, despite the creaking shutter at the window and the shadowy shapes that seemed to be lurking in every corner. Telling myself firmly that the large batlike form on the other side of the room was probably only the cook's apron flung over a chair, I tiptoed across the cracked linoleum and groped in the dark for the refrigerator handle. There it was—no, that was only a drawer—there! I slid my hand along the refrigerator's cold metal surface, found the handle, and pulled. . . .

Light poured out, flooding the kitchen and momentarily blinding me. I blinked, holding my eyes closed for a few seconds to give them a chance to adjust. Then I opened them, ready to peer eagerly into the refrigerator. What treat would I find? A leftover chicken leg? A couple of slices of bread? A jar of mayonnaise? Maybe even a leaf or two of lettuce to make a really elegant chicken sandwich? I could feel my mouth watering in happy anticipation.

But what I saw was not a chicken leg, not the bread I craved, the lettuce, or even the jar of mayonnaise. Smack in the middle of the center shelf was a large tin can, open, with this sign taped to it:

DO NOT TOUCH!
PROPERTY OF COUNT DRACULA!!

That did it!

Back to bed I ran, my hunger forgotten, and pulled the covers close around me. Count Dracula. King of all vampires. THE vampire! I shuddered, thinking of what I had thought was the cook's apron. Of course it hadn't moved, hadn't come slowly toward me, cape outstretched, long teeth gleaming—

Or had it?

The next morning it was easy for me to laugh at my fears, for that's when I met the Count Dracula who owned the opened can. He was a large, jet black cat belonging to a young couple who also worked at the theater. They had always been so fascinated by vampire stories that they had named their cat after the famous blood-drinking Transylvanian Count.

It was through them that I, too, became interested in vampires. If it hadn't been for them and for their feline Count Dracula, I probably would never have written this book. Thank you, Jane and Jay and Dracula, wherever you are!

A thank-you also to Joel Lamon and Diana Miller for telling me about porphyria, a rare disease no doubt responsible for some vampire legends. And to the staff of the Boston Athenaeum for their assistance in finding books.

A special thank-you goes to the late Montague Summers who probably knew more about vampires than anyone else before or since. Mr. Summers, I am told, used to do research in the British Museum armed with a briefcase with the word VAMPIRES written on it in blood red letters! His books *The Vampire in Europe* and *The Vampire, His Kith and Kin* (published in the United States by University Books, Inc. and in England by Routledge & Kegan Paul Ltd.) were a tremendous help to me.

Nancy Garden

1972

1

A THIRST FOR BLOOD

Picture an old-fashioned nursery in a lonely Austrian castle —dark wood furniture, mysteriously dim corners, brown patches of damp on the walls. To complete the picture, a tiny golden-haired girl asleep in a huge, ornately carved bed.

The curtains stir at the window—even though it is closed against the "harmful night air." Suddenly a beautiful lady appears beside the child's bed, her hair long and silky, her dress falling in graceful folds, her slender hands reaching gently out toward the child. . . .

Well, maybe not quite *gently*. And maybe her face is a trifle thin, her teeth—especially the canine teeth—unusually long. Nevertheless, when the child wakes and looks up, alarmed, at seeing a stranger, the beautiful lady dazzles her with a lovely smile and climbs into bed next to her, taking her in her arms. The child, who has no mother, snuggles up to the lady cozily, and breathes a contented, sleepy sigh.

For a moment, the nursery is again quiet and undisturbed.

Then the beautiful lady, with a languid, graceful motion, lifts her head. She gently pushes back the little girl's golden hair, bends down—and bares her long pointed teeth over the innocent child.

So begins *Carmilla*, a vampire story to end all vampire stories, written by Sheridan Le Fanu and published in 1872. Le Fanu knew his vampires well; his characters and plot are unusually faithful to the details set forth in the old folk legends from which all vampire stories come.

As the story continues, Laura grows up and one day meets a girl very like the lady in her childhood dream. This girl, Carmilla, is left at the castle by her mother—a strange, dark woman—after a coach accident. She and Laura become fast friends. However, unlike other girls, Carmilla will say nothing about her past; she never gets out of bed till afternoon; she eats very little; and she has great contempt for anything to do with church and religion. She also looks strikingly like a portrait that hangs in the castle. The portrait is of a lady named Mircalla, Countess of Karnstein, who lived in the 1600s. Oddest of all, however, is Carmilla's attitude toward Laura. "You must come with me, loving me, to death," Carmilla tells Laura. And, earlier, "Think me not cruel. . . . I live in your warm life, and you shall die—die, sweetly die —into mine." Unsettling words, these, especially spoken by a friend!

Not too long after Carmilla's arrival, a young peasant girl in the area dies of a strange wasting disease. Then another dies, and another. Laura herself starts feeling ill and begins to have bad dreams—at least they seem to be dreams. It is whispered that a woman's ghost now walks regularly near the castle. Laura herself sees a catlike creature one night in her room and a few nights later sees Carmilla herself, her nightgown covered with blood.

Despite all this, Carmilla continues to profess the most ardent and possessive affection for Laura. As for Laura, she is torn between her feeling for Carmilla—who is the only friend she has ever had—and her growing certainty that something is wrong, terribly wrong, with the strange girl.

Eventually, a general, friend of Laura's father, pays the castle a visit. His daughter has recently died a mysterious death, and he is trying to find out its cause. To complete his research, the General must go to the ruins of the Karnsteins' home, near where Laura and her father live. Karnstein, of course, is the name of the lady in the portrait whom Carmilla so closely resembles.

By the time the General arrives, Laura is very ill indeed, and growing weaker every day. She is not so ill, though, that she cannot hear the bizarre story the General has to tell. Not long before his own child died, he says, he met a strange dark-clad woman at a ball. "She begged me," the General explains, "to take in her daughter Millarca, as she had to go on an urgent journey and Millarca was not well." With growing alarm, Laura and her father hear how Millarca and the General's daughter became fast friends, how the General's daughter fell mysteriously ill, and then, despite the best doctors available, grew weaker and weaker until she finally died.

Shortly after telling this story, the General sets off for the Karnstein ruins, despite the warning of a local woodman who tells him the ruins are haunted by a vampire. Laura, her father, and Carmilla accompany him. The woodman joins them at the ruins to serve as guide.

When Carmilla meets the woodman, however, to everyone's

horror, her ordinarily sweet expression abruptly changes to one of starkest cruelty. The woodman, with a terrible cry, picks up his hatchet and swings it violently at Carmilla. But Carmilla grabs his wrist and somehow with one dainty weak-looking hand manages to overcome him. In an instant, she vanishes and the General, his face the color of ashes, orders Laura to leave the ruins immediately.

The next day, the General sends for a priest and several medical men. He takes them to the ruins and has them open the Karnstein tomb. A horrifying sight greets them: Carmilla, lying in seven inches of blood! At that point, the General realizes she is also Millarca, friend of his dead child—and the lady in the castle's portrait: Mircalla, Countess Karnstein.

The Countess has been dead for more than a century, but, amazingly, her corpse shows absolutely no sign of decay. In fact, there is even a slight heartbeat and a faint, shallow breathing. The experts around the tomb can draw only one conclusion: Laura's strange, pale friend was not a living girl at all but a universally feared creature with ghastly powers—a vampire.

Shaken as they are, the handful of men carry out the ancient ritual necessary for destroying a vampire. They drive a stake through the heart of Carmilla alias Millarca alias Mircalla. Then they cut her head off, burn her body, and throw the ashes into a nearby river. No more vampire haunts the Karnsteins' tomb, no more local peasant girls die slow, lingering deaths, and Laura is left in peace except for her disturbing memories.

Facing page: Le Vampire, *1857 engraving. Graveyards, cemeteries, and tombs are the usual habitats of vampires, who sleep in their coffins by day.*

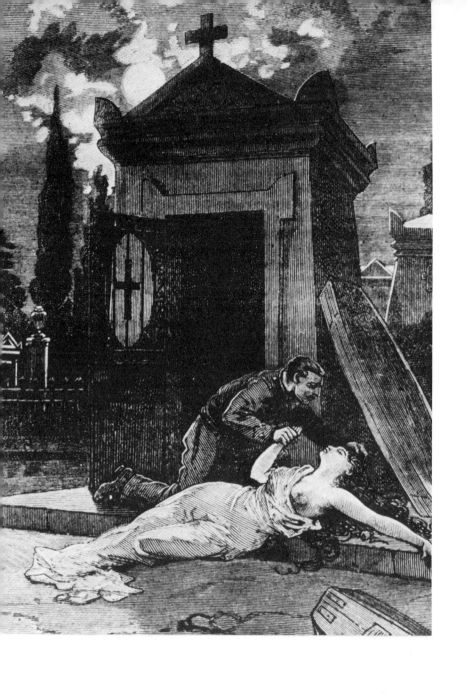

Laura's prolonged illness and the slow deaths suffered by the peasant girls were of course due to Carmilla's method of attack, characteristic of vampires everywhere. The attacking vampire bends down, almost as if it were going to kiss its victim. But instead of kissing, the vampire pulls his lips back, exposing his long teeth, and makes two swift punctures, usually on the left side of the victim's neck. These punctures are very small and neat, and lead directly into the jugular vein. The victim's blood flows freely from the wound, and the vampire drinks it as fast as it flows.

Sometimes a vampire drinks so much blood that his victim dies immediately. But more often, the vampire drinks only enough to satisfy one night's thirst. He then returns when he next feels the need for living blood. The victim (usually, but not always, of the opposite sex) grows continuously paler and weaker day by day. Because most vampires put their victims into a kind of trance before attacking, the victim usually has only the vaguest memories of the attack. Doctors are summoned, but can find no evidence of disease, no explanation for their patient's steadily weakening condition. Occasionally a doctor, church official, or other expert, noticing two tiny puncture marks in the patient's throat, suspects the truth, but usually the patient dies before anyone realizes what is going on. This is especially dangerous because anyone killed by a vampire is doomed to become a vampire himself after death and, unless destroyed, will spend an eternity seeking rich, warm, human blood.

As *Carmilla* suggests, vampires have been around for a long, long time. They go further back in history than most people realize—back even before the seventeenth-century Countess Mircalla of Karnstein. For example, the Chaldeans, who lived near the Euphrates River in southwestern Asia more than five hundred years before Christ, feared vampires or vampirelike creatures enough to have devised charms against them. The Assyrians and Babylonians, even earlier, feared a ghostly creature called an Ekimmu. People whose bodies were not properly buried or who did not have food buried with them could become Ekimmus, and were doomed to wander the earth searching for food. The food which they found, if not actually human blood, was often human vitality. If an Ekimmu entered your house (and, vampirelike, it could even though you locked all doors and windows) your family would all grow weak and sick and would probably die.

In Syria and Palestine, there were definitely creatures who drank human blood; references to them appear on ancient carved tablets. In ancient Ireland, people feared terrible creatures called "red-blood-suckers" and put piles of stones on their graves to keep them from coming out—as people later put tombstones over graves to control ghosts.

In ancient times, when man had no knowledge of biology except what he observed, blood must have seemed a magical substance. To lose a little of this powerful red liquid was of no account—but to lose a lot was to die. Mysterious though the workings of this must have seemed, man soon figured out that blood was essential for life. From that he developed the idea that it *was* life, or at least the source of life. So it must have seemed very logical to feed one's ancestors blood, no doubt in order to sustain their existence after death. Primitive man even fed his crops with this life-giving liquid. This practice added to his belief in the power of blood, for the blood acted as a fertilizer and enriched the soil in which crops were grown.

Man's awe of blood continued into "civilized" times. Frequently popular superstitions and rituals centered around the drinking of blood—certainly a vampirelike thing to do. In Homer's famous ancient epic poem the *Odyssey*, the ghosts in Hades cannot talk until they have had blood to drink. Christ's disciples at the Last Supper were told that the wine they drank was his blood; and in communion services today the liquid drunk by the faithful stands for the blood of Christ.

In later times, blood was sometimes drunk as a sign of love or friendship. A bridegroom in Brittany, France, might drink blood from a small cut he made in his wife's skin. This was believed to create an especially strong bond between the newly

I. N. J.
Dissertatio
HISTORICO-PHILOSOPHICA
De
MASTICATIONE
MORTUORUM,
Quam
Dei & Superiorum indultu,
in illuftri Academ. Lipf.
fiftent
PRÆSES
M. PHILIPPUS Rohr / Marckran-
ftadio-Mifnic.
&
RESPONDENS
BENJAMIN FRIZSCHIUS, Mufilaviâ-Mifnicus,
Alumni Electorales.
ad diem XVI. Augufti Ann. M. DC. LXXIX.
H. L. Q. C.

LIPSIÆ,
Typis MICHAELIS VOGTII.
DE MASTICATIONE MORTUORUM
By Philip Rohr

Strange sounds coming from graves (often because people had mistakenly been buried alive) led to vampire legends and to the belief that the dead sometimes chewed and ate their shrouds and parts of their own bodies. Here is the frontispiece to a lecture on this subject given at the University of Leipzig in 1679.

married couple. Young men in German youth clubs used to seal their friendships by mingling their blood—much the way Indian and white "blood brothers" did in the United States. Blood was also sometimes drunk for nourishment as animal blood—meat juice and broth—still is.

Blood has also been used as a cosmetic. During the Italian Renaissance (fourteenth through sixteenth centuries), some women rubbed blood on their faces to prevent wrinkles. One of the most horrible "vampires" of all time was the sixteenth-century Hungarian countess Erzsébet Bathory, who killed six hundred young girls partly in order to bathe in their blood. She was eventually tried and imprisoned for life in her own castle, the very place where she had committed her terrible crimes. She died behind the thick castle walls—and as far as anyone knows, remained quietly in her grave like any other corpse.

Bathory was not a "real" vampire, for she was alive when she indulged in her mania for blood. True vampires are not alive.

Nor are they dead.

II

BEING—AND BECOMING—UNDEAD

No other creature, no matter how horrible or strange, can claim, as vampires can, to be "undead." Werewolves—those terrifying people who can shift into wolf shape—are certainly very much alive. Man-made monsters like Frankenstein's have life given to them, though not in the ordinary way. Ghosts and other spirits are dead. But vampires are neither one nor the other; they are halfway in between. They have gone through what has appeared to be an ordinary human death, but their bodies remain solid and continue to crave nourishment.

During the day, a vampire lies motionless in its coffin, which must either be buried in his native land or contain earth dug from it. His body may be swollen, ruddy, and plump with the blood of his victims; his skin may be stretched tight as that of a drum. He may have gorged himself so much that his coffin is full of overflowing blood—or he may have had such bad "hunting" that his body is shriveled and thin. Regardless of the amount of blood he has consumed, however, the vampire is apparently dead.

Some, upon close examination, may be seen to be breathing slightly; others show no life signs at all. Breathing or not, bloody or not, all vampires have one thing in common as they lie in their coffins—their bodies, unlike those of truly dead people, never decompose.

When night falls, the vampire stirs, coming out of his grave in the form of a thin mist able to penetrate even the tiniest crack. If mist is not to his liking, he digs his way out. Or if, as was believed in remote parts of Russia, his hands are too numb for digging, he uses his mouth instead.

Once the vampire is out of his grave, it is even more obvious that there is something strange about him. He is, for one thing, unnaturally pale (Chinese vampires are greenish, covered with grave mold, and sometimes glow in the dark). His bright red lips, contrasting sharply with his ashen complexion, barely hide his protruding, cruelly pointed canine teeth. His undead breath smells foul and his eyes burn a diabolical red. Wearing the shroud he was buried in—or, like the famous vampire Dracula, his regular clothes—he travels through the night to his chosen victim, makes his attack, and then returns, before sunrise, to his grave.

There are other signs that instantly say "vampire" to people who know what to look for. Hair and eye color, for example. In many Christian countries, red hair was considered to be a sign of vampirism. This is probably because Judas Iscariot, who betrayed Christ, supposedly had red hair. Eye color was another sign. Vampires in Greece, where most people have dark eyes, were said to be blue-eyed. Rumanian vampires had gray eyes, and Irish ones, black.

Most vampires were creatures of the night only, doomed to fall into instant decay if the sun's rays touched them. But some—

NIGHT FALLS AT COLLINWOOD... AND THE MORTAL REMAINS OF BARNABAS COLLINS RISES FROM HIS SLEEP OF THE *UNDEAD*...

Barnabas Collins was the vampire-hero of Dark Shadows, *a recent TV soap opera and comic strip based on vampire (and werewolf) traditions.*

like Carmilla—seemed immune to the sun, and were considered especially terrifying because they were less vulnerable. Nighttime vampires were often the masters of savage wolf packs, or could order flies, rats, and other potentially harmful creatures to do anything they asked. Most vampires could also take on the shape of any creature they wished. Many chose to be either bats or wolves. Those who chose wolf shape were frequently considered to be part werewolf.

In Greece and Normandy, France, as well as elsewhere, people who were werewolves—or evildoers—in life usually became vampires after death. Any disturbed grave, the Norman French thought, held a former werewolf. They would dig up the corpse, cut off its head, and hurl the body into the sea or a river, presumably believing that this would keep it from becoming a vampire. Dead evildoers in Normandy were believed to eat the clothes they were buried in. Then, howling and screaming, they would burst forth from their graves, often in wolf shape, giving off a greenish glow and a terrible smell.

Gypsies in Poland, Hungary, and Russia were said to have believed in a connection between werewolves and vampires that is stranger still. Anyone born between the new and full moon was thought to be in constant danger of attack by a certain kind of witch who needed the blood of such people in order to live. A person attacked by this blood-sucking witch would gradually grow pale and weak. Then he would start howling like a wolf and finally turn into one. As a wolf, he would grow strong again and soon become leader of a pack, ordering his lesser servant-wolves to hunt for him. This unfortunate creature was unable to drink anything but blood or eat anything but raw meat.

Sometimes the werewolf-vampire connection became very

27

mixed up indeed—as in this story about a man who should probably have been a vampire but was believed to be a werewolf instead:

"King John was not a good man," wrote A. A. Milne in his poetry book *Now We Are Six.* A lot of people back in thirteenth-century England felt exactly the same way. King John Lackland, he was called—"Lackland" because his father hadn't given him as much land as he'd given his brothers. John came to the English throne after the death of his brother, King Richard. But John, unlike Richard, did not have the respect for the power of the church that English kings were expected to have—as a matter of fact, he had so little that he was excommunicated—cut off from the church entirely—as a punishment. John wanted power of his own, but Richard had left him little money. To get more, John taxed his subjects heavily. Those who felt the bite of his taxes liked him as little as the church authorities did—perhaps less.

The circumstances of John's death in 1216 were somewhat mysterious. Some people say he was poisoned; others say he fell fatally ill as a result of overeating. In any case, after he died, strange rumors began to circulate. John had been buried in a cathedral, near two shrines, and it was bandied about that he was unable, since he "was not a good man," to rest in such a holy place. People claimed to have heard ear-splitting shrieks coming from John's burial place, along with weird chatterings and other ghostly noises. At last the church authorities took John's body out

Facing page: King John of England. Because he was "not a good man," he was thought by some people to have returned, vampirelike, from his grave.

of its coffin—so one story goes—and buried it without ceremony in unconsecrated ground. The noises stopped then, but the rumors didn't. Now it was whispered that John had become a werewolf and that in that terrifying shape he could continue to prey evilly upon his subjects.

Since King John was dead, and werewolves were almost always living creatures, one would be right in expecting him to have turned into a vampire instead of a werewolf. But folklore and superstition aren't always completely logical. One part of the King John story is more consistent with legend, however: King John was evil, and an overwhelming majority of werewolves *and* vampires were certainly that!

It was a generally accepted folk belief that an evil being had no soul. Some tribal peoples have believed that souls could be "captured" on film or in mirrors. Other people believed that mirrors revealed people's souls, even if they did not actually capture them. A soulless being, therefore, could be recognized by his lack of a reflection. Anyone who had given his soul to the Devil—as werewolves frequently did—could be found out by leading him past a still pool or holding a mirror in front of him. A vampire was considered equally soulless, even though only some vampires had anything to do with the Devil. (The famous movie *Dracula*, discussed more in Chapter VI, contains a spine-chilling scene in which Count Dracula's true nature is revealed by the fact that he casts no reflection in a silver box.)

Vampires did not all come to their undead state by being unusually wicked or by being killed by other vampires. In Bulgaria, for example, a tendency to vampirism was inherited. Elsewhere, vampires were believed to be the offspring of a witch and the

Devil. In some places, anyone who ate a sheep that a wolf had killed would eventually become a vampire. And a person excommunicated from the church, especially in Greece, was almost certain to become a vampire.

This last is perhaps the source of the widespread idea that vampires did not decompose in their graves, for in Greece it was believed that the bodies of excommunicants did not decompose either. Excommunicants nearly always became vampires so there is clearly some kind of connection here, although it is difficult to figure out which caused which!

Those who committed suicide, which was considered a sin by the church, were often believed to become vampires after death. Suicides were customarily put into running water or buried at a crossroads. The latter was not only to keep them out of hallowed ground, but also so that they would not know in which direction to look for victims if they emerged from their graves as vampires.

No doubt the soullessness of evildoers, plus the fact that suicides, excommunicants, and other wicked people were said to become vampires, contributed to the widely accepted belief in Christian countries that vampires shunned all religious objects. There were exceptions to this—the Slavs had an especially bold vampire who liked to swing playfully on wayside crosses—but, in general, religious pictures, crosses, holy water, and anything else connected with the church was like poison to vampires. The movie industry carried this to such an extreme that most of Hollywood's vampires could be frightened away by a mere cross-shaped shadow, and painfully burned or even destroyed by a few drops of holy water!

Anyone who, according to church law, had been buried incorrectly, was also likely to become a vampire. A certain Hungarian woman, for example, was buried in her local church's cemetery—even though, since she had not received the last rites, she should not have been. A few days later there was a terrible storm. A ghost began attacking the inhabitants of the woman's village, seizing them by the throat. Each person or animal attacked suffered great pain and, later, extreme weakness. For months the attacks continued, and the inhabitants were convinced that they were the victims of a vampire. The prime suspect: you guessed it, the poor woman in the churchyard.

In some places, especially Sicily and Greece, vampires were creatures of revenge. A murdered man whose killer had not been punished could come forth angrily from his grave as a vampire and not rest in peace until his murderer had been killed by one of his close relatives. Any relative who refused to do the deed would himself be doomed to vampirism.

Parental curses were bad, too. A person cursed in a certain way by his parents could turn into a vampire after death. Woe betide the wayward son whose father said to him in anger, "May the ground reject thee!" (In other words, may your body not decompose—the same thing as wishing him to become a vampire.) Evil though they were, such curses could be undone, though a repentant person had to wait till he was dying before he had the chance. Then all he had to do was sprinkle his son—or anyone else he'd cursed—with salt water while saying "I absolve you" or words to that effect. Then his son said "I forgive you" and the curse was dissolved. If the accursed was dead (and presumably already a vampire) removing the curse was a little more difficult. But things could be put right if a piece of cloth with which the

Superstitions about burial and about spirits rising from their graves formed the basis for many a vampire scare. (Engraving by George Cruikshank.)

accursed had been buried was burned in the room of the dying "curser."

Another strange cause of vampirism which many people believed in had to do with cats. If a cat jumped over the body of a dead person, the dead person would become a vampire. People believed this in places as far apart as Greece, China, and Scotland.

There were other unlucky things that could make a person into a vampire, according to folk beliefs in various parts of the world:

being attacked by a vampire

dying unbaptized

committing perjury or lying about another person

being born the seventh girl or the seventh boy in a row to the same parents (such children were also thought to be born with little tails). In some places, though, especially in Britain, being the seventh boy or girl was lucky. A seventh child there was thought to have magic powers which allowed him to heal the sick.

being born on or around Christmas (this could make one a werewolf too, or a werewolf in life and a vampire after death)

being born with teeth

being born with a caul (membrane)

having chorea (a disease characterized by uncontrolled twitching)

being drowned or dying by violence

If a vampire gave the evil eye to a pregnant woman, her baby would be doomed to vampirism, unless the spell was lifted by the church. If a pregnant woman didn't want salt on her food, it was thought that her baby would be a vampire.

34

Now that you've decided that practically everyone you know is doomed to become a vampire, here's one consolation. According to the residents of Yorkshire, England, at some early point in their history, anyone born on a Saturday had nothing whatsoever to fear. Not only could he never become a vampire—he could also never become a vampire's victim!

III

VAMPIRE CHARACTERISTICS

There were as many different kinds of vampires as there were methods of becoming them—maybe more. The Bulgarian vampire, for example, had only one nostril. He came out of his grave nine days after death in the form of a shower of sparks. For forty nights he remained in this form, playing practical jokes, but then he resumed human shape and was ready to do serious vampiristic harm.

Some Russian vampires sucked blood directly from their victims' hearts instead of from their necks. Russian Tartars believed in a vampire who occasionally tried to make a meal of the sun, moon, and stars. This poor creature was never able to satisfy his heavenly hunger, for the stars were so hot he always had to spit the whole meal out!

The usual kind of Greek vampire (there were several), the vrykolakas, was sometimes a mischievous creature, known for his hunger for normal food like eggs as well as for human blood. However, he sucked blood, too, and when he did, he usually lay on top of his victim, sometimes suffocating him. Like most other vampires, the vrykolakas doomed his victims to become vrykolakas themselves.

The word *vrykolakas* was used to mean werewolf as well as vampire, logical when you remember that Greek werewolves became vampires after death. In some parts of Greece, if many children in one family died one right after the other and there was one child who lived despite weakness or deformity, that child was thought to be a vrykolakas. In Macedonia, Greece, it was believed that a special kind of vrykolakas leapt onto the backs of sheep and cattle to suck them dry of blood. "Vampire killers" armed with pointed iron rods or sticks were sometimes hired to get rid of them.

A Greek island called Santorin or Santorini was so well-known for its vrykolakas that bodies of those suspected of being vampires were sometimes sent there from other parts of Greece. The idea was that the people there knew more about destroying vampires than those anywhere else, since they'd had so much practice.

Vampires sometimes were sensitive and choosy about their victims—as is shown in this story set in California near the turn of the century:

Mr. and Mrs. Walsingham and their children had only been in their newly acquired house three weeks when strange things began happening. The doorbell would ring when there was no one outside. Shrieks and laughter disturbed their rest at night. The Walsinghams' daughter, while combing her hair one evening, was terrified to both feel and see a man's hand on her arm —but there was no reflection but her own in the mirror she was

37

The most famous vampire of them all, Dracula, in a weak moment: his true nature is revealed because he casts no shadow in a shiny silver box.

facing. The last straw, though, came one night at dinner, when the Walsinghams had company. Suddenly there was an agonized groan upstairs and great drops of blood began falling from the ceiling onto the Walsinghams' best tablecloth. Some of the party rushed upstairs, but found no sign of anything unusual—even when they stood right over the spot from which the blood continued to drip downstairs.

That was enough for the Walsinghams; they moved out immediately. But a young man who had heard of the bizarre events made a bet that he would not be afraid to spend a night alone in the haunted house.

At first, he had little trouble withstanding the ghostly pranks. A lamp was mysteriously extinguished; the fire in the grate was put out—but he had expected such goings-on. The shrieks and laughter, however, put his nerves more on edge than he had expected. Finally he could stand them no more, so he flung open the door and tried to run outside. Something grabbed his ankle, and then he felt cold fingers closing around his throat. . . .

The young man was found the next morning, alive but in shock, with fingermarks and scratches on his throat. For weeks he lay weak and pale in bed, and no one was able to find any medical explanation for the sudden case of anemia he had developed. The only explanation that seemed to fit the entire chain of events was that the house was occupied by a vampire or family of vampires in whose home the Walsinghams had been unwelcome, although innocent, guests. The Walsinghams had meant the vampires no harm so no real harm was done to them—but the young man, who had insulted the vampires by saying they couldn't frighten him, had come in for harsher treatment.

Jealousy often motivated vampire attacks. In Russia, a certain cruel provincial governor once fell in love with a pretty girl who happened to be engaged to someone else. Since she wouldn't break her engagement, he used his political power to force her to marry him. Never was a wife more unhappy or a husband so cruel; he did not allow her to go out, he beat her—and, even as he lay dying, he made her promise never to remarry. "If you do," he said in a terrible voice, "I will come back and I will kill you."

After a while the memory of those words faded and the young widow again became engaged to her former fiancé. At last, she began to feel some of the happiness which she had been denied for so long. But one night her servants found her unconscious in her room, her body covered with bruises and a tiny bleeding puncture wound in her neck. At the same time, they heard the sound of a coach driving rapidly away from the house.

When the girl came to she told them she had been attacked by her dead husband.

The next night one of the servants saw a black coach pulled by six dark horses rattling furiously away from the house. No one could stop it to question its driver. Meanwhile, inside the house the girl again lay unconscious, blood oozing from her throat. Night after night the same thing happened, and day after day the young widow grew weaker. Medicine did no good; prayers did not help; exorcisms (ceremonies to get rid of ghosts) had no effect—even when performed by the archbishop himself.

One night a band of Cossack horsemen succeeded in stopping the coach, but only for a moment. For one thing, they were so horrified to hear the voice of the dead governor call out to them from the coach that they were stunned. For another, they

Prominent canine teeth are a dead giveaway of a vampire.

were convinced that some power beyond their own fear had temporarily paralyzed them.

At last, though with great reluctance, the archbishop decided to treat the governor's corpse like that of a vampire. It was good he did, for when it was dug up it was found to be undecomposed and full of blood. Blood spurted out when a stake was driven through the vampire's heart. With a chilling shriek, the evil creature expired—leaving his young widow at peace at last.

41

Another jealous vampire, this one in Vienna, Austria, in the nineteenth century, had a different motive for his attacks: money. This evil being was the miserly uncle of a lovely young girl who was married to an ambitious and hard-working—but not prosperous—young man. She herself was an heiress, but through some legal device her uncle had gained control over all her money and refused to give any of it up. As a result, the young couple often had to borrow from friends in order to pay for simple necessities like food and essential clothes.

The old man was ill, however, with consumption, as tuberculosis was called in those days (probably because it caused its victims to waste away slowly as if they were being consumed or eaten away). He finally arranged to leave to the young couple a pitifully small sum of money when he died—far less than what the girl herself was rightfully entitled to. With many regrets, for it seemed unkind even when faced with such a miser, the couple hired a lawyer to see if there was any way to get the girl's inheritance back. The old uncle got wind of this new development and was so angry he vowed to kill the lawyer if he ever had the chance.

Not long after that, the lawyer fell seriously ill. Despite all the doctors could do, he grew steadily thinner till it was feared he would simply waste away into death. Toward the end, the doctors reported sadly that the lawyer's keen mind had begun to crack. He was under the delusion, they said, that some strange old man was visiting him regularly in the night. He held fast to this belief until the day he died.

Meanwhile, as the lawyer languished away, news came to the young couple that the girl's old uncle had miraculously recovered from consumption. He grew stronger every day; he was gaining weight, and his skin had become young-looking and healthy. It was truly an amazing recovery; no one could explain it.

Then came the lawyer's death. Almost immediately, the uncle suffered a relapse. The bloom of health was replaced by the pallor of illness; his weight dropped sharply and, within days, he died.

As for the girl's inheritance, it is not known whether she ever got it. Perhaps she did. Or perhaps, after living through such a nightmare, she was just as happy to do without it!

Not all vampires were harmful, although most were. On that vampire-ridden Greek island of Santorini, for example, there was an occasional good one—a creature doomed to vampirism who nonetheless did kindly deeds in his undead state. One of these "good" vampires looked after his wife and children long after his death, even cutting wood for them and lugging water from the village well. Eventually, though, he had to stop; the neighbors got nervous.

Some vampires were part ghoul (ghouls are creatures who eat corpses). Those Russian vampires who ate their way out of their graves, for example, had very unvampirelike appetites. While still in their graves, they would eat some of their own flesh. Then they would nibble on corpses in neighboring graves. Finally they would prey on the living as did other vampires—except they attacked babies first and then older people.

Ghoulish vampires were most common in India, Arabia, Africa, and the Middle East. Here is a story about one who lived near Baghdad, Iraq, in the fifteenth century:

Abdul-Hassan, son of a wealthy merchant, was of an age to

be married. His father, anxious to have a grandchild, arranged a marriage for him. Abdul-Hassan was a dutiful son and wished to please his father—but when he saw a portrait of his intended bride, he begged for time to think things over.

What troubled young Abdul-Hassan was that the bride his father had found for him was ugly. It did not matter to him that her father, like his own, was a rich merchant and that they would be able to live in ease and comfort, never wanting for a thing. There were things more important than money in Abdul-Hassan's eyes; one of them was beauty. How could he bear to look at an ugly woman all the days of his life, and lie next to her night after night?

For weeks, Abdul-Hassan tried to think of a way of telling his father he would have to refuse this match. He was not sure his father would agree with him that beauty was important in a wife. "If she is virtuous," Abdul-Hassan could hear his father say, "it matters not that she is a little plain. You may be sure then that no other man will look at her."

Pondering this, Abdul-Hassan found he could not sleep and took to walking the countryside near his home. One night, as if in a dream, he heard the gentle, romantic strumming of a lute and a clear, lilting female voice softly singing. He followed the sound to a small, walled-in house and then caught his breath in wonder— for there, on a balcony, was the most beautiful young woman he had ever seen. Her face was as lovely as the sounds made by her voice.

Abdul-Hassan stayed hidden near the wall till the lady went inside. The next morning, he went to the marketplace to an old man who was said to know everyone in Baghdad.

"Who lives in the small house with the balcony?" he asked.

"The one with the wall around it—about halfway up this road?"

"Ah," said the old man, "that is the house of the most learned philosopher in Baghdad."

"And," said Abdul-Hassan, trying to appear casual, "has he a daughter?"

The old man nodded. "Yes; her name is Nadilla," he replied, "and she too is learned, beyond all other women. Poor child; her father cannot give her a fit dowry, so she is as yet unmarried."

Abdul-Hassan needed no more encouragement. What need had he or his father of a large dowry, when they already had more money than they could spend? Breathlessly, Abdul-Hassan hurried home.

His father listened carefully to his story and at length agreed to ask the philosopher for his daughter's hand. Soon all was agreed, and Abdul-Hassan, happiest of grooms, was married to his lovely Nadilla.

It was not long before a shadow fell on the marriage, however. For the first few days of wedded life, Nadilla did not eat, and Abdul-Hassan put it down to a young bride's delicate nerves. But when a week had gone by and he had not seen her taste a morsel of food, he asked, "Dearest, can it be that you are ill? If so, please tell me, and I will get you a doctor. If the dishes served are not to your liking, I will get you anything you crave."

But Nadilla only smiled and said, "Do not worry, husband; I shall not starve. I am not used to eating heartily. Unlike you, I come from a frugal house, and I grew up with little appetite."

Abdul-Hassan decided to accept her explanation for the time being, but he continued to worry.

His worry became panic when he woke one night to find Nadilla had left his side. Abdul-Hassan lay awake until the sun had

45

Vampire, by Edvard Munch, 1895. Many vampires preyed on members of the opposite sex. First the victim was lured in an almost romantic way, then sent into a trance, and finally, attacked.

almost risen; it was not until then that his wife returned. He pretended to be peacefully asleep when she crept back into bed, but he resolved to stay awake the next night and see what he could see.

Somehow Abdul-Hassan got through the following day. He

went to bed as usual and lay feigning sleep while he waited for Nadilla to rise and leave their bed. Rise she did, putting on a black cloak, and then she went out into the night. With a grim sense of foreboding, Abdul-Hassan followed her.

It was all he could do to slip behind her into a lonely cemetery that he, like everyone else in Baghdad, knew was haunted. It was harder still for him to follow her into the tomb she entered and watch her warmly greet a band of ugly, deformed ghouls. Abdul-Hassan shuddered as he saw the lovely Nadilla sit merrily down at table with these ghastly creatures. He felt sick as he watched her dine eagerly upon a recently buried corpse till blood dripped down her chin and human flesh clung to her nails. Unable to watch any more, Abdul-Hassan fled back to his house and went to bed.

In the morning when he woke, he was sure of one thing: he could no longer love Nadilla, since she was clearly a horrible monster and not the sweet gentle woman she had seemed to be.

"You will eat with me," he said to her that night in steely tones. "You are my wife, and it is your duty."

"I will sit with you," Nadilla said soothingly, "but eat with you I cannot."

"True," cried Abdul-Hassan, able to control himself no longer. "You cannot eat with me for you eat with ghouls. You have no appetite for decent food, for you feed on human flesh and blood!"

Nadilla made no reply, but she grew pale and went swiftly from the room. Later that night, when Abdul-Hassan lay in a fitful sleep, Nadilla bent over him in cold fury and ripped open a vein in his neck. Greedily, holding him down with a knee on his chest, she drank his blood. Abdul-Hassan woke in pain and

47

wrenched free of his ghoulish vampire wife. He drew the poniard he had carefully placed by his bedside and stabbed her swiftly until she died—or seemed to.

Three nights later, however, Abdul-Hassan woke to find Nadilla draining him of blood once again. Again, he managed to escape. The next day, he ordered her tomb opened—and there she lay, breathing slightly, her mouth and clothes covered with blood. Luckily, Abdul-Hassan knew well what to do: he had a huge funeral pyre built and burned the undead corpse upon it. She never bothered him again.

Sometimes, vampires share characteristics with ghosts instead of ghouls. There are numerous folk stories of people being chased or teased by shroud-clad creatures who never show the slightest interest in drinking human blood. Yet the storytellers call these beings vampires rather than ghosts. One reason for this may be purely due to vocabulary. In some languages, as in Greek with the word for vampire and werewolf, one word is used to refer to any number of supernatural creatures.

The question of the exact identity of any individual night-creature is perhaps best left up to the people who encounter it. There was little doubt, for example, in the minds of the Irish country folk in the following story that the creature they were dealing with was a vampire, even though it may never have tasted a drop of human blood:

A quiet Irish priest, respected but not loved by his parishioners, died suddenly at the age of fifty. His body was taken outside the parish to his mother's house so it would be nearer the family plot in the mountain graveyard where it was to be laid to rest.

The priest's mother, grief-stricken, decided after the funeral to stay at home instead of going to the burial. Her son had been her pride and joy and she wished to mourn him in private.

The graveyard was some distance outside the village, so the burial party did not linger there, being anxious to get home before dark. Hurry though they did, it was sunset by the time they drew near home again. The road was a lonely one and traveled only rarely—almost never at night—so the members of the party were surprised to see a dark-clad man hurrying toward them as they approached the village. The man, they soon saw, was a priest and, though certainly a priest might well have business at any hour of the day or night, it seemed unlikely for one to be going toward the deserted graveyard instead of toward the village where there were people who might have summoned him.

When the priest caught up to the burial party, he turned his head aside and walked faster. But he was not quick enough. They saw that he was *the man they had just come from burying!*

He was dreadfully changed, the frightened people agreed; his skin was ghostly pale and his lips were fuller and redder than they had been in life. His eyes glittered like the coldest of metals and his teeth—his teeth were as long and as sharp as a wolf's.

The frightened people rushed headlong into their village and went straight to the bereaved mother's house. With sinking hearts they pounded on her door. No answer. No sound. No sign of life.

Finally one man put his face close against the window and peered in.

"She's dead," he told the anxious villagers. "She's lying there on the floor, dead. He must have gotten her, or else she died of fright."

49

"We must make sure," another man said, putting his shoulder to the locked door to force it open.

It was a good thing he did, for the priest's mother was only unconscious, not dead. When she came to she described to them the same ghostly version of her son that they had seen on the road. She had fainted, she said, when she recognized him through the window.

Ghost or vampire—that's hard to say. The dead priest certainly looked like a vampire, yet he apparently did not drink his mother's blood. That would seem to make him a ghost.

Unless, of course, his mother had something around the house that automatically repelled vampires.

IV

HOW TO WARD OFF A VAMPIRE

In the early eighteenth century in the village of Kisolova, Yugoslavia, a certain man died in what seemed to be a normal way. But a few days later he appeared as a ghost to his shocked family. "Give me food," he demanded. "I am hungry." His son, terrified, served him a meal; the ghost ate heartily and went away. Two nights later, however, he came back, again demanding food. This time his son was not so frightened, and he was angry at being ordered to give up food needed by the living. "Go away," he told the ghost boldly. "I have no food to spare."

The ghost left—but the next morning the son was found dead. That very day several other people in the village got sick, all with the same mysterious symptoms: weakness, listlessness, pallor—but no fever and no pain as with other illnesses. There was another "symptom," too, though no one dared speak of it out loud: all of the sick people had had the same frightening dream— a dream in which the dead man had come to them in the night, bitten them in the throat, and sucked out great quantities of blood.

Nothing helped these poor sick people, though the desperate villagers tried everything they knew. Despite all their herbs and soups and fine nursing, nine people died within the same week.

The village magistrate appealed to a nearby city for help, and was sent not doctors, but the Commander of the Army, who brought some of his officers with him, plus the public executioner. These men marched straight to the graveyard—while all the village trembled behind closed shutters and locked doors— and bravely opened the dead man's grave.

It was as they had suspected. The man lay as if in a trance. His face was ruddy and full, not pale and sunken as a true corpse's would have been. He appeared to be well fed, his mouth was smeared with fresh blood, and he was breathing slightly. The public executioner finished off the undead man with the usual vampire-killing technique, that of pounding a stake through his heart and then burning the body. Next, the Commander had his men dig up the bodies of the vampire's victims. So far they looked dead instead of undead, so they were not staked, but bunches of garlic were put in their coffins as a precaution before they were reburied.

This vampire-discourager—garlic—was one of the most widely used all over the world. Worn around the neck, placed in vases in a room, tied in bunches to doors, or rubbed around windows and other entrances, it gave unfailing protection against vampires. Garlic placed in a vampire's grave would prevent the undead corpse from emerging. As recently as 1912, a Hungarian farmer was reported to have stuffed a corpse's mouth with garlic, presumably because he suspected it of being a vampire.

Religious objects, as we have already seen, were strong protection against vampires in Christian countries. A person who wore a cross around his neck could never be harmed by a vampire. A vampire buried with a cross could not rise from his grave.

In Poland, to protect themselves from attack by vampires, people ate bread made from flour and the blood that flowed from a staked or decapitated vampire corpse. Elsewhere, vampires

A cross, in most Christian countries, keeps a threatening vampire at a distance.

feared light; some recoiled from iron—so leaving a victim's room brilliantly lit or barring his door with iron sometimes kept vampires away.

Corpses suspected of having a tendency to vampirism could be protected in various ways. In Dalmatia, Yugoslavia, corpses were wounded so they would be unable to walk if they became vampires. In Burma, the toes were tied to the thumbs for the same reason; elsewhere, the feet were tied together. In parts of Finland, the corpse was nailed to its coffin to keep it from emerging as a vampire. In some remote parts of Greece, people who were afraid they might become vampires sometimes asked their children to stake and burn them after they had died, just in case. Cremation instead of burial was a preventative also, although in some places and at some times church authorities disapproved, wishing to allow bodies of the faithful to decompose naturally. Putting a piece of communion wafer into a corpse's mouth was also considered effective. It was believed by Christians that this would prevent any evil spirit from entering the dead body. Money in the mouth was another method, used in parts of Germany— perhaps a carry-over from the ancient belief that one had to pay Charon, the ferryman of the River Styx, in order to get safely into Hades, land of the dead.

Burial at a crossroads, as for suicides, was another means of prevention. In addition to confusing the vampire, a crossroads, it was thought, would remind him of the cross of Christ and therefore keep him from coming out of his grave. One could also bury a vampire deeper than a normal person in order to make it harder for him to dig out—but this was probably no more effective than burying him face down.

Since people in many countries believed that a vampire corpse did not decompose, forced decomposition became a widespread means of prevention. In China, for example, the corpse of anyone likely to become a vampire was left unburied until the decomposition process was well advanced. In parts of Rumania and Greece, it was believed that a person's soul couldn't leave his

54

body until forty days after death—so everyone, good or bad, was in danger of becoming a vampire for the first forty days after dying. For that reason, corpses were dug up periodically to see how far decomposition had advanced. A body which was not completely decomposed after the right length of time (this varied, depending on the age of the person at death) was treated like a vampire's. Once it was completely decomposed, though, a body was treated with great respect. Its bones were thoroughly washed by the dead person's relatives, and reburied with appropriate religious ceremonies.

In Yugoslavia, if a person suspected that a recently deceased friend was a vampire, he would always make sure to take a sprig of hawthorn with him when he paid his condolence call on the surviving relatives. When he left, the caller would drop the hawthorn in the street outside the house, believing that this would distract any following vampires long enough for him to escape.

As the hawthorn trick shows, even though vampires are diabolically purposeful in their attacks, they can be easily diverted if one uses the right methods. Grain and seeds of various kinds were used for this purpose in many countries. A vampire, the theory goes, will always stop to count each kernel or each seed he encounters (why he does this no one seems to know). If enough is scattered, the vampire will not be finished counting by dawn and will be destroyed or made powerless by the light of the sun. For this reason, people in eastern Europe scattered grain over corpses suspected of being vampires. If their suspicion were true, the vampire would be so occupied each night in counting the grain that he would never be able to escape his grave. In China, rice was scattered around a vampire's grave after he had left it for the night. The returning vampire would stop to count and so would be caught and destroyed by the rising sun. For the same purpose, in many countries grain was scattered on the roofs and thresholds of homes of potential victims.

In Czechoslovakia, especially on Walpurgis Night (a little like Halloween), people protected their cows and other farm animals by putting thorny branches on the floors of their barns. Any vampires or witches who came to disturb the animals would get caught on the thorns before they could do any harm.

Occasionally people were able to control vampires because the undead warned their victims of their presence. The Greek burculacas did this. He was the body of a wicked, often excommunicated person, who, instead of decaying in the grave, would swell up so much that his skin sounded like a drum if thumped. He visited people at night, calling their names. Anyone who answered would die on the next day. The vrykolakas, the more familiar Greek vampire, would sometimes call its victims, too, but this vampire could not call more than once. Anyone who didn't answer the first time was safe.

A "calling" vampire turned up in Wales in the Middle Ages —odd, because there were practically no vampire legends in the British Isles until sometime later. But this story, recorded in the twelfth or thirteenth century, tells of an evil man who died and returned four nights later to haunt his village. He would stand outside his neighbors' cottages and call them by name three times. Within a few days, whoever he had called sickened and died.

A knight told the bishop about this and the bishop suggested digging up the body and cutting off its head with a spade. Then, he said, the grave should be sprinkled with holy water and the body reburied.

All this was carefully done, but the vampire somehow fastened his head back on and continued to call and kill his neighbors. Finally, when there was practically no one left alive, the vampire visited the knight. This worthy waited until the third call faded away outside, and then he rushed out and split the creature's skull with his sword. That was the end of that.

Which only goes to show that an unorthodox method can sometimes work, even with vampires.

V

VAMPIRE DISPOSAL

Because a vampire is neither dead nor alive, he can only be destroyed by special methods. These methods have always varied from country to country.

Step one, however, was usually to locate the vampire's grave. Sometimes a few holes above the grave gave the main clue, at least when one was dealing with those vampires who dug their way out. Sometimes, too, people were already pretty sure who the local vampire was and could go straight to the right grave. But in other cases, more elaborate means had to be employed. In Hungary, for example, a young, virgin boy was made to ride to the graveyard on a coal black (in some villages, snow white) equally young and innocent stallion. He had to ride carefully among the graves, walking the horse over each one. At one grave, the horse would stop and refuse to go farther. That was the grave where the vampire lay.

In Russia a vampire could sometimes be tracked to his grave.

To do this, someone simply scattered salt on the floor of the victim's room. The salt would stick to the vampire's feet and make a clear trail to his daytime resting place. Sometimes also, as in this nineteenth-century story, a vampire could be followed to his hiding place:

An Englishwoman and her two brothers rented a fine old country house known as Croglin Grange. It was near a churchyard and, unlike most houses in the area, had its bedrooms on the ground floor. The three moved in as the countryside drew in upon itself for winter. As far as anyone knew, they were well satisfied with their new home. But in late spring, when the weather suddenly turned hot, they had a cruel shock which made them think twice about their choice of location.

One night all three stayed up as late as they could for it was too hot to sleep. When at last they went to their rooms the sister opened her window to get what little air was circulating. It was still too hot to sleep, so she lay in bed lazily watching the progress of the night. Just as she grew drowsy, she noticed two lights moving toward the house from the direction of the churchyard. She watched them sleepily for a while, and then snapped awake as she realized they were not lights at all but eyes—eyes attached to a darkly looming body which moved steadily closer to her open window. At the last minute she shook off her fright enough to spring out of bed and run out of the room, but at that moment *it* appeared at her window—a paralyzingly ugly face with burning, evil eyes.

The woman watched helplessly as the creature climbed in through the window, and she was powerless, too terrified to scream, as it grabbed her and bent her head back. Then, as its cruel teeth bit into her throat, the sudden pain freed her voice and she screamed, loud and clear.

Although no more than a minute or two passed before her brothers burst into her room, the creature had jumped out of the window and was already running through the Grange's garden toward the churchyard. The brothers chased it over the wall, but were unable to catch it. As for the woman, she recovered and, being a sensible sort, was soon able to convince herself that there

Croglin Grange, site of one of the strangest vampire stories of all time.

was a logical explanation for what had happened to her—some poor soul escaped from a mental hospital, she told herself; certainly nothing supernatural; such things did not exist outside of popular novels. Nevertheless, all three members of the little family decided it would not be a bad idea for them to distract themselves from the memory of their ordeal, so they closed up the house for the summer and went off to Switzerland.

By the time fall came, though, the sister decided it was time to return; why take a house, she reasoned, if you do not live in it. So they all three went back to England and once again spent a cozy, peaceful winter in Croglin Grange.

One spring night, when they had all pushed the horrible incident of nearly a year before into the backs of their minds, the sister was awakened by a scratching sound on her window (which she now was always sure to keep shut). She awoke and sleepily stared into the darkness. Suddenly the clouds broke outside; moonlight framed the window—and once more, the woman screamed, for there in the window was the ghastly creature with the burning eyes.

This time, although the creature again escaped, the brothers were more successful in their chase. One of them managed to shoot the creature in the leg just as it leapt over the churchyard wall.

There was no doubt now as to where the creature came from, and little as to what it was. The next day the brothers and several neighbors marched grimly to the churchyard and opened the ancient burial vault. The sight that greeted them was so horrifying they almost fled: every single coffin—but one—had been broken into and all the corpses, sacrilegiously mutilated, lay about on the floor.

The men bent to their grisly task. Hammer and chisel resounded in the silent vault; the one intact coffin, age sealed, now sprung open—and there was the ghastly creature who had visited Croglin Grange—with a fresh pistol wound in its leg.

The ugly corpse was shriveled, perhaps because its attack on the woman had been unsuccessful. The brave men soon reduced it to ashes and the residents of Croglin Grange lived out their quiet lives in peace from then on.

As in the Croglin Grange story, one of the most common methods of destroying a vampire was by burning. Staking was another, and was often combined with burning. The stake (in Albania, a dagger) had to be driven through the vampire's heart to fasten him firmly to the ground. Usually the stake had to be made of wood, and often the wood had to be of a particular kind. Aspen, which was believed by some people to have been the wood used in Christ's cross, was often used. So was ash, and so was whitethorn; it depended on what the local superstitions were. Vampires nearly always yelled when the stake was driven in, and blood spurted out of the wound in great quantities.

Usually this unpleasant operation had to take place at dawn, right after the vampire had returned from his nightly feast. In parts of Greece and Turkey, it could only take place on Saturday, for that was the only day the creature was sure to be in his

Facing page: Practically the only surefire method of destroying a vampire forever was to drive a wooden stake through its heart. This one shouldn't be a bother anymore.

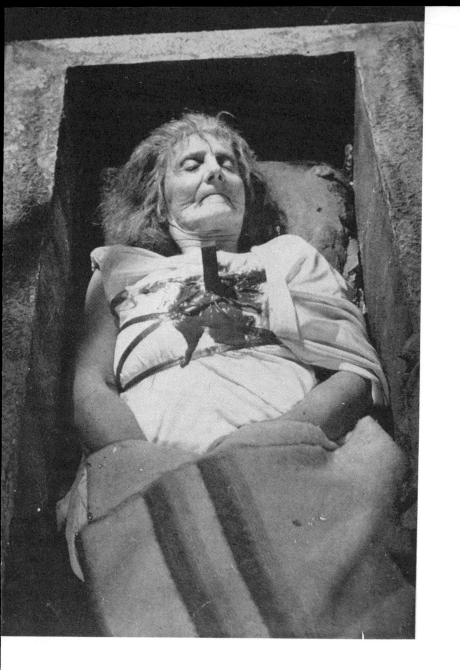

grave. It was believed that since Saturday, the day after Christ died, was sacred to the Virgin Mary, no vampire could leave his grave on that day.

In some places—the Balkans, for example—instead of a stake or a dagger driven through the heart, a nail had to be driven into the skull. Then a wild rose branch was put on the vampire's chest so if by any chance he was still able to get up he would get tangled in the thorns and wouldn't be able to move.

A vampire might turn to dust as soon as he had been staked. But it was often necessary to take extra precautions to be sure he was really dead. After staking, the vampire's head would be cut off—with the church sexton's spade if possible—and his body burned or hacked to bits and then burned. To make even surer that he would not return, his heart could be removed, treated with vinegar and oil, and torn up. Then boiling water, boiling oil, or holy water was poured into the grave.

No matter how a vampire was destroyed, though, it was always important to be successful in the first attempt. Vampires "slept" with their eyes open, so they were well aware of who their killers or potential killers were. Anyone who failed was likely to find himself the vampire's next victim. But terrifying as the prospect of failure was, it was worth the risk. A vampire who was not destroyed was likely to live on indefinitely, preying on people generation after generation—like this one:

A certain French nobleman had been spared the ravages of the French Revolution (1789–1799), when the peasants rose up and overthrew the nobility. He was an unusually thin man with sharp teeth that protruded from his mouth. What is more, he was well known for his cruelty. After the Revolution he did not try to hide his distaste for the peasant-citizens who now ran the country—a distaste so deep and bitter it led him to commit murder over and over again. Eventually the nobleman himself was murdered by the friends of his many victims.

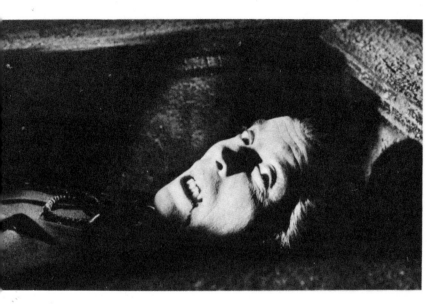

Vampires traditionally slept with their eyes open, which meant anyone who set out to destroy one had to do the job right the first time!

Not long after he was buried, however, a young peasant child in the area died, with two tiny puncture marks in his throat. Then another died, and another. The deaths continued, unexplained, for years, and increased sharply during a short period of time when repairs were being made to the tomb in which the nobleman's body lay.

After seventy-two years of this, the nobleman's grandson put all the facts together and came up with a pretty good—if frightening—explanation. He begged a priest to open the tomb—and was not particularly surprised to see that, unlike all the other corpses there, his grandfather's body was as smooth and whole as if he had died the day before. When a stout whitethorn stake was pounded into his heart, fresh blood poured out; the nobleman's final undead scream shook the entire tomb. The body was burned and the heroic grandson and his neighbors joyously celebrated an end to three-quarters of a century of vampiristic killings.

It wasn't always absolutely necessary to go to such extremes to dispose of a vampire. A vampire could, for example, simply be turned over in his grave. This wasn't a foolproof method, but there was at least a chance that when the creature tried to dig out of his grave, he'd go in the wrong direction.

People along the eastern shore of the Mediterranean believed that vampires—like witches and werewolves—were unable to cross water. In that case, it was simple to get rid of them. All you had to do was take a vampire's body to an uninhabited island and dump it there. No messy staking, no ghastly shrieks in the local graveyard, none of the gore and bother usually associated with vampire killing. Of course terrible moans came from these vampire "dumps" all the same, as the hungry undead creatures paced angrily back and forth from sunset till dawn.

In some Slavic countries, you could kill a vampire neatly by shooting him with a silver bullet. There were a couple of complications, though. For one thing, the bullet had to be blessed by a priest. For another, you had to keep the vampire's body, after shooting him, out of the moonlight. If the moon's rays hit the body, the vampire would revive.

Bulgarian vampires, who were inclined to swell up the way the Greek burculacas did, could sometimes be destroyed by pricking them to let the gases causing the swelling leak out. But elsewhere other methods had to be used. One of the most ingenious of these, which seems to have been practiced only in Bulgaria, was bottling.

There were certain magicians who were known as professional vampire-bottlers. They would bait a bottle with the vampire's favorite food (presumably human blood) and try to drive him into it. More often than not, the vampire would attempt escape by climbing the nearest tree. Undaunted, the magician would follow, forcing him into the bottle by threatening him with a holy picture. Faced with human blood on one side and a holy picture on the other, the vampire would have no choice but to turn toward the blood. When the vampire was safely in the bottle, ecstatically licking up the bait, the magician would whip out a cork and ram the bottle shut. The vampire, furious, would try to escape—only to be driven back by the cork, which had another holy picture cleverly pasted on its underside.

Triumphantly, the magician would take the bottled vampire off to the villagers who had agreed to pay him—handsomely—for his services. A fire would have already been prepared, and the magician would throw the bottle, vampire and all, into its blazing flames.

Among gypsies, especially in Balkan countries such as Yugoslavia, Rumania, Albania, and Turkey, magicians weren't enough.

Their vampires were invisible to ordinary people, and so were unusually hard to kill. The only people who could kill them (and see them) were dhampirs—children born of vampire fathers and gypsy mothers. The gypsy mothers may not have been too anxious to get rid of their vampire husbands, however, for they were especially helpful when it came to household chores. For some reason these gypsy vampires kindly helped their wives in any task which involved thread—weaving or sewing, for example. Nevertheless, they were inveterate cattle killers and so had to be destroyed. (One gypsy vampire was said to have killed a herd of forty in one summer—as recently as 1946.)

To destroy one of these gypsy vampires, one must call in a dhampir, usually his own son. The dhampir then goes through a complicated ritual in public. First he blows his nose and looks to north, south, east, and west. He then whistles, and darts about as if hunting someone. (In the meantime, the spectators who have gathered keep their distance, for they have been warned that if a single drop of blood falls on them during the ritual they will go insane and then die.) The dhampir then strips to his underwear and, holding up his shirt, peers through its sleeve as if looking a great way off. "What shape is the vampire in?" asks the crowd, usually by this time in a near-hypnotic trance from observing this rite. The dhampir replies that the vampire is in bird—or snake or human—shape, or whatever shape, indeed, he believes it to be. Then, suddenly, he seems to meet the vampire face to face.

Facing page: Vampire-destroyers were sometimes well-paid professionals. However, the job was usually done by courageous clergymen, doctors, or ordinary people.

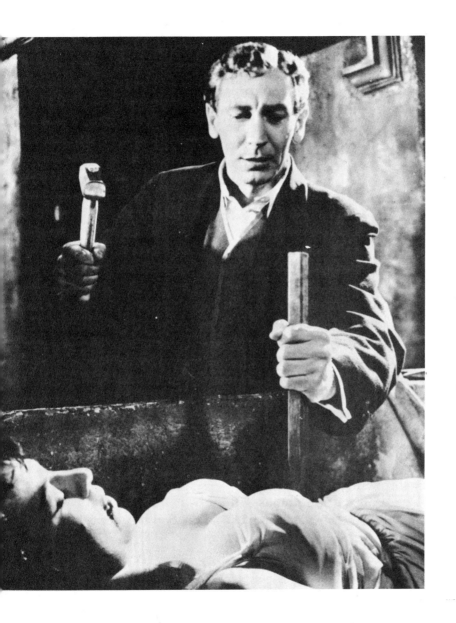

Quickly, he attacks. As the fight progresses, the dhampir struggles so vividly against his unseen foe that the spectators are sure they see the vampire clearly. At last the dhampir, with a triumphant whistle, straightens up and announces he has killed the vampire. No one can dispute him, for everyone knows that no one but a dhampir can see a vampire.

Despite the fact that this ritual seems like something out of the dark ages it has been practiced well into modern times. A vampire-killing by a dhampir was reported somewhere in the Balkans only fourteen years ago. Though old-fashioned dhampirs accepted payment for their services in livestock or clothing, modern ones also take money—and the most enlightened are said to fight their vampire fathers with guns as well as with fists!

A dhampir fighting against his father—a faithful nurse barricading her charge's bedroom with garlic and crosses—a silent band of grim-faced men meeting in a cemetery to stake, decapitate, and burn a vampire—this is surely the raw material of melodrama. It is no wonder, then, that fiction writers seized eagerly upon the vampire legend. Many an author, from ancient times to the present, has molded the old tales to suit his own purposes. Some have invented details of their own; some have combined many legends in one new work; some have used the bare bones of folklore to create new vampires and vampire myths. Whatever the method, though, the result—poem, play, book, or movie—has rarely failed to find a fascinated audience.

VI

DRACULA'S ANCESTORS

Not too many people would disagree with the statement that Dracula is the most famous fictional vampire of all time. The black-caped Transylvanian Count, created by author Bram Stoker, has made his chilling undead way through more books, stories, plays, movies, and comic books than any other vampire. Toy cars have been named for him; play teeth and bats have been modeled after him; his picture has appeared on stickers, notebooks, and even cereal boxes. There are clubs devoted to his memory, and tours booked to his castle in Transylvania. He hasn't yet had his one hundredth anniversary—and won't for more than twenty years—but all signs point to his surviving as a favorite horror character long beyond that time and in many countries of the world. Before the book *Dracula* was published in 1897, vampires were of many different kinds, as we have seen. After *Dracula*, so powerful was Stoker's tale, all vampires tended to be very like the famous Count.

Nonetheless, Stoker drew heavily on ancient vampire legends when writing about the Count. He also took careful note of the works of other writers of vampire stories—Le Fanu, for example. Carmilla is probably Dracula's closest female ancestor in literature. His closest male one was created even earlier, and the details of his character were developed by several writers before Stoker adapted him into the familiar dashing, cape-clad Count.

It all started in the summer of 1816 in Switzerland. A small group of friends—the English poet Percy Bysshe Shelley, his wife-to-be Mary Godwin, the poet George Gordon Byron, and his doctor-companion John Polidori—were spending their summer vacation together. The only trouble was, the weather was terrible—it rained day after day after day, and the friends, unable to walk in the beautiful Swiss countryside, decided to pass the time by swapping stories. They began by reading ghost stories aloud, but then decided to make up their own. The most famous tale to come out of that attempt to relieve boredom was Mary Shelley's *Frankenstein*—but the other major one, more famous in its descendant *Dracula* than in itself, was John Polidori's *The Vampyre.*

Polidori didn't have the original idea for *The Vampyre*; Byron did. But Byron never finished his story. Polidori changed a few things in the fragment Byron wrote, and added many of his own to make a complete short novel.

In Polidori's tale, the Dracula-type character is named Lord

Facing page: Frontispiece to Varney the Vampire, *popular novel of 1847.*

No. 1.]   Nos. 2, 3 and 4 are Presented, Gratis, with this No.   [Price 1d.

VARNEY THE VAMPIRE

OR THE

FEAST OF BLOOD

A ROMANCE OF EXCITING INTEREST.

BY THE AUTHOR OF
"GRACE RIVERS; OR, THE MERCHANT'S DAUGHTER."

LONDON: E. LLOYD, SALISBURY-SQUARE, AND ALL BOOKSELLERS.

Ruthven. He is a pale man with disturbing gray eyes, who takes a young man named Aubrey on a "world tour." (It was usual, in those days, for young people to be taken on such trips as part of their education.) Aubrey soon learns that Lord Ruthven is a desperate gambler and a ruthless cad who leaves a trail of empty purses and broken hearts wherever he goes. After a while Aubrey decides he's had enough of this sort of thing so he strikes off on his own and goes to Greece.

There he falls in love with Ianthe, a pretty young girl who tells him about vampires. When he dismisses her stories as nonsense, she becomes frightened, saying that people who don't believe in vampires are sure to be hurt by them. Aubrey does feel uneasy when, in describing what a vampire looks like, Ianthe lists features very like Lord Ruthven's—but he is still sure the whole thing is only groundless superstition.

One evening at dusk, Aubrey finds himself deep in a wood which he has been warned to avoid. Ianthe and her parents have told him vampires meet there. He tries to convince himself there is nothing to fear, but, nevertheless, when a thunderstorm develops, he is grateful for the excuse to take shelter in a small hut which is conveniently near his path. Eagerly, he hurries toward it—but his blood runs cold when a woman suddenly screams inside. He rushes in, and before he even has time to look around, someone or something grabs him brutally around the throat. Luckily a party of horsemen burst in just in time to save his life. But no one can save the lady whose clothes are covered with blood and whose slender neck is marred with toothmarks. The lady, alas, is Aubrey's beloved Ianthe.

Aubrey, half mad with grief, picks up and pockets a dagger he finds near the body, perhaps with some thought of later using it for evidence. It is a beautiful instrument, heavily carved with a design unlike anything he has ever seen.

A long time passes before Aubrey is able to think of trying to find his beloved's murderer. He falls gravely ill soon after that horrible night. Almost as if summoned to his former companion's bedside, Lord Ruthven appears and offers to nurse Aubrey back to health. At first Aubrey cannot bear to look at him, much less be cared for by him, but he is too weak to protest. He slowly grows accustomed to Ruthven again, and by the time he has recovered Aubrey has forgotten his dislike of Ruthven enough to agree to travel with him once more.

Not long after they start out, the two companions are ambushed by a band of robbers. Lord Ruthven is gravely wounded in the fight—so gravely that he prepares to die. "Don't tell anyone of my death," he says to Aubrey, "for a year and a day. And take my body to a mountaintop where the moon can shine on it tonight."

Ruthven dies, and Aubrey carries his body to the top of a mountain and leaves it. The next day he returns to give it a proper burial—but the body is gone. He tries to shrug off the mystery and tells himself there must be a logical explanation, but later, when he sorts through Ruthven's belongings in order to dispose of them, he finds a sheath covered with oddly familiar carvings. With a sinking heart he compares the carvings with those on the dagger he found in the hut where Ianthe was murdered. Not only do they match perfectly, but the dagger also slips easily into the sheath—so easily it is obvious they were made for each other.

The connection between Ruthven and Ianthe's murder is now clear, but Aubrey tells himself that since Ruthven is dead

THE VAMPIRE:

OR, THE BRIDE OF THE ISLES,

A ROMANTIC MELO DRAMA,

In Two Acts,

BY J. R. PLANCHE, Esq.,

Author of the Merchant's Wedding, A Woman never Vext,
The Brigand, Amoroso, The Mason of Buda,
A Daughter to Marry, London and Paris, Vampire, &c.

PRINTED FROM THE ACTING COPY, WITH REMARKS,
BIOGRAPHICAL AND CRITICAL, BY D.—G.

To which are added

A DESCRIPTION OF THE COSTUME,—CAST OF THE CHARACTERS,—
ENTRANCES AND EXITS,—RELATIVE POSITIONS OF THE
PERFORMERS ON THE STAGE, AND THE WHOLE
OF THE STAGE BUSINESS,

As performed at the

THEATRE ROYAL, LONDON.

EMBELLISHED WITH A FINE ENGRAVING,
By MR. BONNER, from a Drawing taken in the Theatre, by
MR. R. CRUIKSHANK.

LONDON:	NEW YORK:
SAMUEL FRENCH,	SAMUEL FRENCH & SON,
PUBLISHER,	PUBLISHERS,
89, STRAND.	122, NASSAU STREET.

Facing page: Title page of the script for a famous vampire play performed in London in the 1820s.

A dramatic scene from the second act of Planché's The Vampire.

there is nothing more to fear. Aubrey goes home to England, determined to forget his unpleasant experiences abroad. For a time he succeeds. Then, at a party given for his younger sister, he sees a man who is so strikingly like Lord Ruthven that Aubrey cannot doubt he has returned, though dead, to haunt him. Soon afterward, Aubrey's sister shows him a picture of someone called Lord Marsden. "I am going to marry him," she tells Aubrey, her eyes glowing with happiness—but Aubrey stares at the picture in stunned silence. It is the man at the party; it is Lord Ruthven all over again. "Don't marry him," he begs his sister. "Don't marry that man; you must not!"

But when the girl asks "Why?" as well she might, the honorable Aubrey remembers his promise to tell no one of Ruthven's death for a year and a day. "I cannot tell you," he whispers hoarsely, "but, oh, my sister, do not marry him."

That, of course, is not a convincing enough answer for a young girl in love, and so the preparations for the wedding go forth as planned. Over and over again Aubrey tries to find ways to warn his sister against Ruthven without breaking his promise; he also tries to stop the wedding—all to no avail. Half mad with frustration and terror, Aubrey dies of a burst blood vessel just before the wedding. And so his innocent sister becomes the evil Lord Ruthven's next victim.

This story was so popular one could almost say it started a vampire craze. All England, it seemed, loved—or at least was fascinated by—a vampire. Writers hastened to feed this fascination and booksellers made sure to keep their latest vampire stories in stock. Actors hastily rehearsed play after gory play. Theater technicians devised a special "vampire trap" to enable stage vampires to disappear mysteriously before the audience's eyes. It consisted of a rubber trapdoor with flaps that opened and closed so quickly and smoothly it really was hard to see—especially when the stage was dimly lit—that the "vampire" had simply fallen through.

One of the best-known vampire plays in England during this "craze" was *The Vampire, or The Bride of the Isles* by J. R. Planché. It was based on a French play which in turn had been based on Polidori's tale. In 1828, Planché adapted the same story for a German opera called *Der Vampyr*. By 1847, people were still interested enough in the subject to buy a book by popular author Thomas Preskett Prest called *Varney the Vampire*—220 chapters and 868 pages long. By 1853, *Varney* was still so popular that it was sold as a "penny dreadful"—in separate parts for a penny apiece. *Varney* certainly had all the right ingredients for a chilling vampire tale—a beautiful young girl, a terrible vampire with "eyes of polished tin," and an atmosphere complete with eerie moonlit nights and terrifying howling gales. The story finally ended when Varney plunged melodramatically into the famous Italian volcano Mount Vesuvius, and was burned from undead to dead.

The next big vampire story in English was *Carmilla* (1872)—and then, in 1897, came the most famous of all:

DRACULA

VII

DRACULA

Count Dracula was by no means a completely made-up character, although most of the details we "know" about him were made up. There was, however, in fifteenth-century Transylvania (part of Rumania) a real soldier and minor ruler known as Vlad Tepes or the Voivode Drackula or Dracul. He governed the small province of Walachia from 1455 to 1462 and again in 1476—governed so ruthlessly that mere mention of his name made his enemies tremble. *Tepes* meant *the impaler*, a nickname the original Dracula acquired because he liked to stick the bodies of people he had executed onto the ends of pointed sticks. This seems to have been more than a passing fancy of his, too—in fact, some sources say that he had a hundred thousand people killed. The province he governed was under Turkish rule, but he didn't get along well with his masters; many Turks were among his victims. Vlad Tepes was a member of an organization called The Order of the Dragon and it may have been the order's dragon symbol that gave him the name "Dracul"—which means both

The real Count Dracula was nicknamed "The Impaler" by his con-temporaries. Here he is shown with some of his many victims. (From a German pamphlet published by Matthias Hupnuff in 1500.)

dragon and devil. The name Dracul later became Dracula, and although its unpleasant owner was certainly not undead, he was nevertheless called a vampire in old Transylvanian records, and was also said to have had dealings with the Devil.

The real Dracula apparently had some psychological reason for his cruelty. As a young boy he had been taken prisoner by the Turks and had been grossly mistreated. Later he had again been jailed, this time by Hungarians. At that point he began to show sadistic tendencies, for he enjoyed torturing small animals and birds brought to him by his guards. A psychologist would probably say this was partly because he himself had been cruelly treated as a boy.

The fictional Dracula, however, was no psychologically unbalanced impaler. He was gloriously supernatural, undead and dashing, more related to his fictional ancestors than to his real one. Bram Stoker, his creator, did know about the real Dracula and set part of his story where the real Dracula had lived. But most of the fictional Dracula's character was a product of Stoker's incredibly fertile imagination.

Bram Stoker, who was born in Ireland in 1847, was sickly as a boy and couldn't walk until he was eight years old. His father was a theater-loving civil servant. His mother, a social reformer, entertained her seven children with tales of her girlhood, often liberally spiced with accounts of fairies and other Irish "little people."

Bram read Le Fanu's *Carmilla* when it came out in 1872, and stored it in the back of his mind. When he finally wrote his own vampire story, it was even more successful than Le Fanu's had been, first as a novel and then later as a play. It wasn't long before all London was thrilling to his magnificently melodramatic

The real *Count Dracula, Vlad Tepes of Transylvania. He was as blood-thirsty as his namesake.*

tale—and then all England, and then America, and soon, much of the rest of the world.

If you stood the fictional Count Dracula next to his creator, you would never mistake them for brothers or even close relatives. Stoker, despite his weakness as a child, had grown up to be a tall, sturdy man, whose robust manner was accentuated by his full reddish beard. The Count, on the other hand, looked far from robust. Here is how Stoker, speaking through the character Jonathan Harker, describes him in *Dracula*:

> . . . a tall old man, clean shaven save for a long white mustache, and clad in black from head to foot, without a single speck of colour about him anywhere. . . . his hand grasped mine with a strength which made me wince, an effect which was not lessened by the fact that it seemed as cold as ice—more like the hand of a dead than a living man. . . . His face was a strong—a very strong—aquiline, with high bridge of the thin nose and peculiarly arched nostrils; with lofty domed forehead, and hair growing scantily round his temples but profusely elsewhere. His eyebrows were very massive, almost meeting over the nose, and with bushy hair that seemed to curl in its own profusion. The mouth, so far as I could see it under the heavy mustache, was fixed and rather cruel-looking, with peculiarly sharp white teeth; these protruded over the lips, whose remarkable ruddiness showed astonishing vitality in a man of his years. For the rest, his ears were pale, and at the tops extremely pointed; the chin was broad and strong, and the cheeks firm though thin. The general effect was one of extraordinary pallor.

*Author Bram Stoker, who created the most popular vampire in history,
Dracula.*

Harker notices other odd things about the Count: that he has hair growing out of his palms and that something, perhaps his bad-smelling breath, makes Harker feel sick whenever the Count moves close to him. He is not made any more comfortable by the wolves howling outside the Count's castle—wolves which the Count affectionately calls "the children of the night," saying, with pleasure, "what music they make!"

The Count himself appears far less often in Stoker's book than one might expect, although his presence is felt on every page. The story is told in diary form by several people who want to know why Lucy Westenra, the best friend of Jonathan Harker's fiancée, is growing paler and sicker day by day. As the small group of friends comes close to the truth, the suspense mounts almost unbearably; no one suspects the Count until close to the end of the book. Finally—but not until Lucy has herself become a vampire—the Count is followed to his Transylvanian home where he is at last destroyed—or so it appears. . . .

Success though it was, Stoker's book was not made into a play until 1923, when an actor-manager named Hamilton Deane finally adapted it. Deane had read the book back in 1899 and thought immediately that it would make an excellent play. When more than twenty years had passed without anyone's making it into one, he finally took on the job himself.

By June of 1924 Deane's play was ready to be performed. If the actors needed any preview of how their opening-night performance might be received, they got it during one of their final rehearsals. A policeman, so the story goes, dropped in at the theater just as the actor playing the Count, bathed in the eerie glow of a green spotlight, rose from his coffin. Rumor had it that no policeman ever turned so pale or ran so fast!

It wasn't long before Deane's play of *Dracula* was a roaring —or maybe a shrieking—success. Audiences in Scotland and in English country towns and small cities loved it. When it finally opened in London, however, Deane had a bitter blow. The first-night critics gave it bad reviews, so bad Deane almost gave up and closed the show. Luckily he didn't, for the audience, as usual, loved it and soon made it a success again despite the critics.

Dracula was now performed so skillfully that people in the audience actually fainted every night. Deane played that up by hiring a nurse to patrol the aisles during the scariest moments. Most nights only about seven people fainted, but one night the nurse was kept extra busy tending twenty-nine who toppled dizzily over in their seats.

Gimmicks were used onstage as well as off—smoke bombs so there could be plenty of mist, whistles and megaphones to make eerie offstage cries, and a battery-run bat with eyes that glowed red. One of the cleverest effects was the old disappearing one. Dracula's coffin had two flaps which the "corpse" was able to close easily over himself when the stake was supposedly pounded through his heart. At the same time a cloud of fuller's earth (like dry clay) was released, hiding the action of the flaps and making it look as if the "corpse" had turned to dust.

By the time *Dracula* was ready for its 250th performance in London's Prince of Wales Theatre, it had already become a success in the United States and Canada. If you had been at the performance at the Prince of Wales on that anniversary night, you would have received a double-barreled present: a book of Stoker's short stories (including a scene written for *Dracula* that had never been published)—plus a toy bat which flew jauntily out of the book when it was opened.

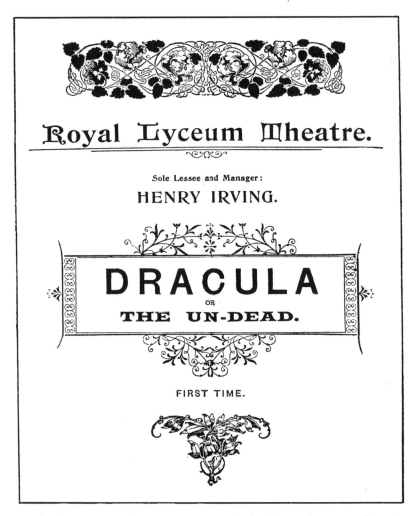

The first stage performance of Bram Stoker's Dracula was a dramatic reading of the book. Its purpose was not so much to entertain as to publicize the author's right to his work and to protect him against violation of copyright.

SYNOPSIS OF SCENERY.

Prologue : Transylvania.

SCENE 1.—Outside the Castle.
    "   2.—The Count's Room.
    "   3.—The same.
    "   4.—The Castle.
    "   5.—The Ladies' Hall.

SCENE 6.—The Count's Room.
    "   7.—The same.
    "   8.—The Chapel Vault.
    "   9.—The Count's Room.

Act I.

SCENE 1.—The Boudoir at Hillingham,
    "   2.—Dr. Seward's Study.
    "   3.—The Churchyard, Whitby.

SCENE 4.—The same—Night.
    "   5.—The same.

Act II.

SCENE 1.—The Boudoir—Hillingham.
    "   2.—The same.
    "   3.—The same.
    "   4.—The same.
    "   5.—Outside Hillingham.
    "   6.—Lucy's Room.
    "   7.—The same.

SCENE 8.—The same.
    "   9.—The same.
    "   10.—Mrs. Harker's Morning Room.
    "   11.—Room in the Berkeley Hotel.
    "   12.—Mrs. Harker's Drawing-Room.
    "   13.—The same.
    "   14.—Outside the North Hospital.

Act III.

SCENE 1.—Lucy's Tomb.
    "   2.—Room in the Berkeley Hotel.

SCENE 3.—Lucy's Tomb.
    "   4.—Outside the Tomb.

Act IV.

SCENE 1.—Room in the Berkeley Hotel.
    "   2.—Dr. Seward's Study.
    "   3.—The same.
    "   4.—Carfax.
    "   5.—Dr. Seward's Study.

SCENE 6.—Renfield's Room.
    "   7.—Mrs. Harker's Room.
    "   8.—Dr. Seward's Study.
    "   9.—Room in the Piccadilly House.
    "   10.—Dr. Seward's Study.

Act V.

SCENE 1.—Dr. Seward's Study.
    "   2.—Room in Hotel—Varna.
    "   3.—Room in Hotel—Galatz.

SCENE 4.—Outside the Castle—·Night.
    "   5.—The same—Before Sunset.

Stage Manager ...   .   Mr. H. J. LOVEDAY.

Musical Director   ...   .   Mr. MEREDITH BALL.

Acting Manager ...   .   Mr. BRAM STOKER.

Because this performance was held primarily for legal reasons, little attempt was made to adapt the book into a workable play. As the number of scenes listed here suggests, the result must have been a long, rather tedious evening at the theater!

LITTLE THEATRE

JOHN STREET, ADELPHI, STRAND

Licensed by the Lord Chamberlain to JOSÉ G. LEVY   Lessee: JOSÉ G. LEVY

MONDAY, FEBRUARY 14th, at 8.30

By arrangement with JOSÉ G. LEVY and HENRY MILLAR

HAMILTON DEANE and H. L. WARBURTON

PRESENT

THE VAMPIRE PLAY

"DRACULA"

By

HAMILTON DEANE

Adapted from BRAM STOKER'S Famous Novel

PROGRAMME

The cover of the program for the first performance of Hamilton Deane's play Dracula, *adapted from Stoker's book.*

ACT I.	..	The Study of Jonathan Harker's House on Hampstead Heath (Evening)
ACT II.	..	Mrs. Harker's Boudoir (Night)
ACT III.	..	The Study of Jonathan Harker's House (Afternoon)
EPILOGUE ..		The Coach House at Carfax (6 p.m.)

There will be an Interval of ten minutes after Act I, twelve minutes after Act II, and no interval between Act III and the Epilogue.

Play produced by HAMILTON DEANE

Furniture by LYON & Co.

General Manager	..	⎫				⎧ ..	ALBERT KAVANAGH
Stage Director ..	..	⎬ For Hamilton Deane and		..	..	LODGE PERCY
Stage Manager ..	..	⎱ H. L. Warburton		..	..	JACK HOWARTH
Assistant Stage Manager	⎭			..	..	BERNARD GUEST

ISABEL HIRSTFIELD, of the Albert Hall and Queen's Hall Concerts, will play selections from the following during the intervals :

1.	Prelude C Minor ...	...	...	...	... Glière
2.	Sonata Tragica	...	...	...	... Macdowell
3.	Preludes ...	...	...	...	... Chopin
4.	Rhapsody	...	...	...	Dohnanyi
5.	Scherzo E flat Minor	...	...	...	Brahms
6.	Fantasie-Impromptu	...	...	...	... Chopin
7.	Danse Rituelle du Feu	...	...	...	de Falla
	(pour chasser les mauvais esprits)				
8.	Hungarian Rhapsody No. 8	...	...	... Liszt
9.	Au Printemps	...	...	...	Grieg
10.	Slovakia ...	...	...	...	... Novak

ERARD GRAND PIANO.

A Bell will ring in the Lounge Two Minutes before the curtain rises.

Manager .. (For José G. Levy & Henry Millar) .. Miss MARY GROVES

EXTRACTS FROM THE RULES MADE BY THE LORD CHAMBERLAIN.—The name of the actual and responsible Manager of the Theatre must be printed on every play bill. The Public can leave the Theatre at the end of the Performance by all exit and entrance doors, which must open outwards.

Where there is a fireproof screen to the proscenium opening, it must be lowered at least once during every Performance to ensure its being in proper working order. Smoking is not permitted in the auditorium. All gangways, passages and staircases must be kept free from chairs or any other obstructions, whether permanent or temporary.

Box Office .. .. .. (Open 10 to 10) .. .. .. E. G. NORMAN

A page from the same program. Note that Dracula *has now been condensed into three acts—two less than in the copyright performance.*

Dracula, the book, went on being popular after it had been adapted once again, this time into a movie. The first film version was made in 1921 by a German director named F. W. Murnau. (There had been one preceding vampire movie: *The Devil's Castle*, made in 1896, one year before Stoker's *Dracula* was published.) Murnau's movie, a silent film called *Nosferatu*, took place in Bremen, Germany, instead of London, England. Dracula's name was Count Orlock, and a few other details were slightly changed, but basically the story was the same. There was one problem, though: *Dracula* was covered by copyright, which meant no one could use the story without permission. Bram Stoker was dead by the time *Nosferatu* was released (he died in 1912), but his widow heard about the movie and sued. The case dragged on for years; during it, the film company lost all its money. In 1925, the court finally reached a decision, and ordered all copies, plus the negatives, of the film destroyed. At least one copy survived, however, for the film later turned up in London and by 1929 had reached the United States.

The first United States-made Dracula movie appeared in 1931. Many others followed; many actors have played Dracula and other vampires in the United States and abroad. But no actor (with the possible exception of England's Christopher Lee) is so closely associated with the part as the star of that first Hollywood Dracula movie, a relatively unknown Hungarian immigrant named Bela Lugosi.

The 1931 movie itself has become a film classic, largely but not exclusively because of Lugosi's performance. The bleak and spooky Transylvanian castle, the spectrally howling wolves, the gray mist and frightened villagers; the stark black and white film and the well-executed camera work all contributed to make this film memorable. But all of this might have been forgotten had it not been for Lugosi himself.

Bela Lugosi had played Dracula in the first United States stage version of the book, so he knew the part well. Although he had had little experience in the United States except for that, he had acted with the Royal National Theater in Hungary and had made movies in Germany.

Lugosi was in his forties when he made the film that was to assure him a permanent place among Hollywood greats. He was tall and dark, with features very like those Stoker described as being Dracula's. In addition to that, he spoke English both on and off screen with an accent, which perhaps made him a more believable Transylvanian than an American actor might have been. His voice had a ghostly hollow ring and his blue eyes, made more piercing for the movie with the assistance of two pinpoints of light, seemed to burn with hypnotic intensity. "I am—Dracula," Lugosi announced in chilling tones near the beginning of the movie—and few people in his audience could doubt it.

Nor, unfortunately, could Lugosi. His fame had a steep price tag attached. He went on to make horror film after horror film (including the famous werewolf movie, *The Wolf Man*). Most of them involved vampires: *The Mark of the Vampire, The Return of the Vampire, House of Dracula*—eventually he even played the Count in a catchall called *Abbott and Costello Meet Frankenstein!* In 1942, he went back to the stage in a revival of the play *Dracula* and in 1951 he toured with it in Britain. By then he had been playing essentially the same part for more than twenty years. Unlike many other actors, he was assured of a sizable, steady income—but unlike many, he was never allowed to be versatile. An actor frequently measures his skill by how many

93

Bela Lugosi played Dracula on the stage before starring in the 1931 Universal film version. In the opinion of his fans, his chilling portrayal of the bloodthirsty Count has never been equaled.

different kinds of characters he can play successfully; Lugosi never had the chance to do that.

When Lugosi came home from his 1951 tour, he began to have trouble getting parts. Vampire movies were still popular, but not popular enough to warrant their being made at the rate they had been in the past. Soon the Hungarian actor was reduced to playing the Count in a nightclub spoof. And not long after that, his fans were saddened to hear that their idol had been a morphine addict for many years, having first taken the drug for severe leg pains. The morphine eventually caught up with Lugosi, especially when it became harder for him to find work. He went into a state hospital for treatment and after he came out he made two more movies. Soon the pains in his legs became so severe that he had to spend most of his time in bed. Mercifully, he died not long afterward, in August of 1956.

Before he died, this man, who looked so much like Dracula and who had played him some two thousand times, asked to be buried in his black Dracula cloak, with its dramatic red satin lining. His wish was carried out—not, one imagines, without some uneasiness on the part of the more superstitious of his attendants.

Funny thing about actors and vampire cloaks. Hamilton Deane had played Dracula, too, in addition to making the first stage adaptation of the book. And when he died, two years after Lugosi, *his* Dracula cloak was found among his ordinary, more conventional clothes. . . .

VIII

ANCIENT AND ODD:
VAMPIRES AROUND THE WORLD

Once upon a time near the ancient Greek city of Corinth, a strong, athletic young man named Menippus met a beautiful woman while he was out walking. "I have been in love with you for a long time," she told him, gazing fondly into his eyes. "Please—come to visit me tonight, and let me sing to you and give you wine to drink."

Of course Menippus went; what young man could resist such an invitation? In fact, he called on the lady many times and before long decided to marry her.

His teacher, the philosopher Apollonius, objected as soon as Menippus made his engagement known. "You cannot marry her," Apollonius said. "She is not the kind of woman one can marry." But, since he wouldn't tell Menippus why, Menippus saw little reason not to go ahead with his plans.

Even though he disapproved of the match, Apollonius attended the wedding feast, which was held in a rich, lavishly decorated hall. Menippus was glad to see him and greeted him warmly. But Apollonius looked suspiciously around the beautiful hall. "Who," he asked, "owns all this gold and silver?"

"Oh," said Menippus, "my bride does; I own nothing but my cloak."

Apollonius shook his head gravely and reminded his pupil of the gardens of Tantalus in Hades, which look real but are not. "Your bride," he said to his angry pupil, "is like that. She is a serpent, a vampire, an empusa, a lamia—a creature who loves you not. She loves your flesh only, and—hear me, Menippus—*she will devour you.*"

"Begone!" shouted the lady at Apollonius from across the hall. To her guests she smiled and laughed. "What nonsense the old man speaks," she said to them, as if apologizing for the odd behavior of an eccentric but harmless guest.

But Apollonius would not leave. Instead he went on talking about the treachery of vampires and as he did the gold and the silver began to melt into nothingness. The lady, weeping, left off trying to impress her guests and begged him to stop. But Apollonius talked ruthlessly on until she at last broke down and confessed that she was indeed an empusa and planned to fatten her young husband up only in order to eat him and drink his blood. Thus, Menippus was saved from disaster.

John Keats (1795–1821), a famous English poet, retold this story with some variations in a poem he called "Lamia." The more usual lamia, though related to the empusa, was a bit different. She preyed especially on children, and seems to have been based on a demon called Lilitu or Lilith, who, according to ancient legend, was the first woman on earth, even before Eve.

Pictures of Lamia or Lilith, probably as charms to protect against her, have been found in ancient Babylonian carvings. There are actually a number of related stories about her, most with the theme of a woman deprived of her children and therefore resentful enough of other women's children to want to destroy them. She was called Lamme or Lamashtu. In Babylonia and Assyria, there were complicated incantations to protect against her ravages; there she was described as a horrible-faced bringer of fevers and disease. Seven similar demons were associated with her, all of whom were especially dangerous to women in childbirth and to young men susceptible to female beauty. She was

Amulets in Hebrew which were hung up to protect newborn infants against Lilith. Note that one is for girls, the other for boys.

also sometimes described as a wolf and a drinker of blood, able to attack anyone from the weakest of infants to the strongest of men.

Like most ancient demons, she had many shapes as well as many names. In one picture, she was shown with characteristics of various animals: dogs, birds, scorpions, men—combined to make up a single horrible monster.

When Lamia passed into Greek mythology, she settled down into a more specific individual. According to the ancient Greeks, she lived in Libya, and had some children fathered by the god Zeus. The goddess Hera, Zeus's wife, was understandably jealous, and killed Lamia's children. Lamia, in bitter revenge, then sought to kill every child she could lay her hands on. Often she drank the blood of the children she killed, and ate their flesh. Although she had once been beautiful, she then became ugly and, perhaps harking back to her earlier monster self, was seen as a serpent and a devourer of men as well as of children.

The story of Lamia passed into ancient Hebrew legend also. In the Talmud (the original book of traditional Jewish law), she was called Lilith and was Adam's first wife. She and Adam had an argument over which one of them was better. Lilith refused to agree submissively that Adam was and, in the end, became so angry that she threatened to leave him. Three angels—called Sanvi, Sansanvi, and Semangelaf—begged her to stay, but she refused.

To punish Lilith for her defiance, her children were killed. Then Eve came along and bore Adam children; Lilith, full of jealousy, tried to kill them. Eve's "children," of course, could be taken to mean all mankind—and, perhaps believing that, people used to wear amulets to protect themselves against Lilith. To be effective, the amulet had to bear the names of the three angels who had tried to make her stay with Adam.

The Lilith story is probably the main link between ancient vampirelike creatures and the modern vampire popularized by Bram Stoker. In the Middle Ages, the story of Lilith and Adam was still told and the names of the three angels were still carved into amulets for protection. Babies were especially vulnerable—girls for the first three weeks of their lives, boys for the first week—as the following story shows.

A happily married knight, in about the twelfth century, was horrified to wake up the morning after the birth of his first son to find that the child had been foully murdered—his throat cut—during the night. The knight recovered from this bitter blow, and by the time his wife became pregnant again he was full of happy expectation about the child he would soon have. But the same thing happened to his second son—and to his third as well.

The fourth time, he was determined that his child would live. The knight and his wife spent months praying and doing good works. The night the child was born, they saw to it that their house was full of people and blazing with light to ward off evil spirits.

The newborn baby, another son, was healthy and rosy, and was laid tenderly by his father in the cradle which had briefly sheltered his poor unfortunate brothers. Faithful friends and relatives guarded the tiny boy all night, determined not to leave him unprotected even for a moment. Even a tired stranger, eloquently begging shelter after a long journey, offered to help guard the child as soon as he saw how things were.

As midnight approached and passed, the faithful watchers

felt a growing sleepiness—all except the stranger. He, too, at last began to nod—but suddenly to his horror he saw a woman enter the room, bend over the cradle, and draw a knife as if to cut the child's throat. Quickly the stranger shouted; the others woke up and the woman was seized. When her veil was put aside, the good villagers were shocked to recognize her as a respected lady of the village, noble of birth and, till now at least, of deed also. "Are you the Lady So-and-So?" the stunned people asked her. "Why have you done this terrible thing?" But their questions were in vain, for the lady bowed her head and would not speak.

"She is ashamed," said the knight at last, still holding his newborn son close to his breast, grateful that he had been spared. "We should let her go; surely she will repent now."

"No, no," said the stranger who had been quiet up until now. "She is a dangerous demon; let me mark her as such." And with a key from the church he branded her on the face. Then he said loudly, "Let the true noble lady be brought." The people turned aside, clucking their tongues, sure now that the stranger was mad even if he had saved the baby's life. But the stranger insisted that the noblewoman be brought, even though to all eyes he held her by the wrist. Finally a servant was sent, schooled in many apologies, to her house.

To everyone's surprise, the servant soon returned—with the noblewoman. She looked in wonder at her double, who now fought against the stranger's grasp. The people gasped as they saw how alike the two were. Both even had the same key mark on the face, though the woman the servant had brought knew not how she had come by hers.

At last the people realized that the first woman was an impostor, and that the noblewoman had not threatened this child or hurt any other. When everyone understood this, the stranger let go of the lamia, for, of course, such was the murderess. With a hideous, piercing screech, she rose like a hawk in the air and flew out the open window.

It is often thought, despite Lamia-Lilith's non-Christian beginnings, that Dracula-type vampires are the products of Christian countries alone. This is by no means true. There were vampires and creatures like them in places where Christianity was not an important religion, or where it was nonexistent.

Chinese vampires, for example, shared many characteristics with their European cousins. Instead of being undead, however, the Chinese vampire was more likely to be an evil spirit who had entered the body of a corpse for the purpose of preying on people—alive or dead, it didn't much matter which. He could fly, as European vampires often could, and he had to limit his activities to the hours between sunset and sunrise. But the Chinese vampire had a tendency to look more like an animal than a human, for he was often covered with hair and had long clawlike nails. Even when he did not look animallike, his victims did not turn into vampires themselves. And he did not always kill them by drinking their blood. . . .

A man once stopped at a crowded inn in China with his three traveling companions. They were all so tired they told the innkeeper they didn't mind where they slept—so they were given the same room in which lay the corpse of the landlord's recently deceased daughter-in-law. The man's three companions fell asleep instantly, but he could not help feeling that something was wrong behind the curtain that separated the four of them from the corpse. Finally he heard a rustling sound and then to his horror the curtain was pulled aside. The pale dead girl went softly up to his friends, leaning over them and exhaling several times. Our hero pulled the covers up over his head lest the corpse breathe on him, too.

When some time had gone by the man cautiously peered out and saw that the corpse had gone back behind the curtain. He got up and tried to wake his companions, meaning to suggest that they would all be better off sleeping outside, but his friends lay as if dead. Horrified, the man turned to flee. No sooner had he left the room than he heard the rustling steps of the girl vampire's corpse hotly pursuing him. His terror grew as the creature gained on him, and at last he realized his only chance was to trick her. Quickly he ducked behind a willow tree. The corpse sped past and the clever man turned and ran off in the opposite direction. But the corpse had caught on. She had turned while the man was still behind the tree, had run back, and now was waiting. With one leap, she had him. The poor man fainted as he fell, but luckily he fell away from the corpse in such a way that she grasped a tree trunk instead of him.

The next morning the man was found, weak but still alive. Nearby lay the ghostly vampire corpse, her clawlike fingers deeply embedded in the bark of the tree which she still clutched.

The other three men? They never woke from their trance-like sleep. They were dead; though the vampire never touched them, her foul breath had been enough to extinguish their lives.

Another type of Chinese vampire was far more spirit than flesh. This was a kind of devil, and appeared in the form of dots of light or a "will-o'-the-wisp"—mist arising from marshes. In rainy periods, this kind of vampire was often seen in cemeteries at night and was said to bring disease and crop failure—as, indeed, excessive rain can do.

In Melanesian folklore there was a vampirelike creature called a talamaur. It was the soul of a dead person who traveled around much as vampires did and lived off the remaining spark of strength in dying or just-dead people.

Malaya had a particularly interesting creature called a pĕnanggalen, who was only a head and stomach, and who sucked the blood of babies, children, and women in childbirth. The pĕnanggalen was always female, though there have been numerous conflicting descriptions of how she came to take such an odd form. Some say she was a vampire soul, descended from a woman who was frightened while sitting in a vat of vinegar—apparently as some kind of religious penance. When a man suddenly came along and asked what she was doing, she tried to run away, and struggled so hard to get out of the vat that her skin split and her stomach, though still attached to her head by the esophagus, became separated from the rest of her body. Other accounts speak of quite a different origin: Once upon a time the pĕnanggalen was a normal woman, who, however, apprenticed herself to the Devil to learn magic. When she learned to fly, her body stayed where it was while her head, neck, and intestines soared into the air to seek food. This pĕnanggalen had to keep a jar of vinegar at home in which to soak her intestines after each night's journey. The intestines apparently tended to swell during the night's adventures; the vinegar shrank them small enough so they could reenter their proper place in the pĕnanggalen's body!

An even more complicated Malayan vampire was the polong and its pet or familiar, the pĕlĕsit. If a sick person, in his delirium, talked about cats, a knowledgeable person would realize he was the victim of a pělěsit and a polong rather than of some ordinary disease. (No one seems to know why talking about cats was a symptom; the polong and pělěsit had nothing to do with cats and did not even look like them!)

The pělěsit was a cricket-demon with a tail sharp enough to burrow into a person's body. The polong looked like a tiny person, male or female, and had the ability to fly. When its pělěsit chirped, letting it know everything was ready, the polong quickly flew to the tunnel made by the pělěsit and through it entered the victim's body.

Not all people, however, were in danger of becoming victims of these creatures. Some people kept both kinds as pets and helpers, using them to attack their enemies. A pělěsit often chose its own human master or mistress, who then treated it regularly to its favorite food—human blood or saffron rice. The polong, however, had to be caught or manufactured.

To make a polong, according to the old tales, all you have to do is collect some blood from a man who has been murdered. Then put the blood in a bottle, and say magic words over it for a week or two. A polong will grow from the blood, and will chirp to let you know when it is ready to come out. You then must cut your finger and put it in the bottle for the polong to suck, and you must do this every day. Then, if you want to harm your enemy, you send your polong off. It will gladly kill your enemy or make him sick or insane by burrowing into him. There is a danger in this, however. Though some polongs will never tell who sent them to do ill to a person, others will. Then the attacked person will recover—and you, as the polong's master or mistress, can of course be punished.

The vampire in Nosferatu, *Murnau's 1922 German film, played by Max Schreck.*

Though pĕlĕsits usually found their own masters, they too could be made if one knew how. The procedure, however, was more complicated than the one used for making a polong. One needed a child's body; it had to have been dead for fewer than forty days. It also had to have been the firstborn child of a firstborn mother. The body then was held above an anthill in the middle of a clearing until it yelled and stuck its tongue out. The tongue was bitten off, put in a coconut shell, and heated over a fire in the middle of a three-road crossing. When oil came out of the shell, the tongue was soaked in it and buried in the middle of the crossing. By the third night after that, if all had been done correctly, the buried tongue would have turned into a pĕlĕsit, which, like the polong, could be used against enemies.

Ashanti folklore, in Africa, tells of a creature similar to the Malayan pĕnanggalen in that it concentrated on sucking the blood of children. The obayifo fed on children until they wasted away and died. It could also suck sap from plants, thus destroying crops. Unlike most vampire-creatures, though, obayifos were abnormally interested in ordinary human food—so people who believed in them were careful never to seem greedy lest their friends suspect them of this kind of vampirism!

Vampirelike creatures were known in the early non-Christian days of the New World, too. In ancient Mexico there were creatures called ciuapipiltin, females with chalk-white faces, arms, and hands, who brought illness to children. There were also ciuateteo, the spirits of women who died while bearing their first babies; they too brought sickness and death to the young. Families with babies used to seal all the cracks in their houses so these lamialike vampires could not enter.

Anyone in Mexico who was a sorcerer was also considered a vampire. In fact, the belief was so widespread that when Spain conquered Mexico and converted it to Christianity, priests used to ask people if they were sorcerers and also if they sucked human blood. Vampire stories must have continued to be popular, however—for today Mexico is among those countries known for making chilling vampire movies.

Vampires were known in the West Indies, too, where they were called loogaroos—which is almost the same as the French term for werewolf, *loup garou*. A loogaroo was an old woman who had made a pact with the Devil. She could shapeshift, if she first removed her own skin, and usually changed into a blob of light. Her main goal in changed shape was to suck human blood. To prevent a loogaroo from entering their houses, people scattered grain outside as in Europe. The loogaroo had to count every kernel and dawn usually rendered her powerless before she was through. West Indian loogaroos shared a certain characteristic with werewolves: if hurt while in loogaroo shape, the same wound always showed when they changed back to human shape. . . .

One morning a West Indian gardener woke up feeling weak and noticed a spot of blood on the clothes he had slept in. He was sure he had been the victim of a loogaroo. The next night he stayed awake and sure enough, he heard a persistent scratching at his roof a little after midnight. He lunged at it with his knife. Something let out a terrible screech and when he looked outside he saw a blob of light fly into the house of a neighbor woman. The next morning that same woman was found nursing a fresh eye injury that could have been made with a knife. She said she had fallen over a stump—but who believed that? No one who knew about loogaroos!

Loogaroo—pĕnanggalen—obayifo—ciuateteo—how much did these non-Christian creatures stem directly from the Judeo-Christian Lilith and her lamia forebears? Perhaps some, but probably not a great deal, for there wasn't much contact from one part of the world to another when these legends first began, especially among the peasants who believed in them. Some legends were certainly carried from place to place by traders and explorers. But there must have been additional reasons why people in widely separated parts of the world believed there were creatures who, after their own deaths, returned to suck the blood and sap the strength of the living.

IX

HOW AND WHY

Before a person can believe in vampires he must believe in ghosts, for anyone who laughs at the idea of dead souls returning to earth is not likely to accept the idea of the undead bursting out of their coffins and sustaining themselves on human blood. People have believed in ghosts at least since the days of ancestor worship, if not before. Back in those days, there was little reason *not* to believe that the state of being dead wasn't very different from the state of being alive. The ancient Egyptians, for example, buried food with their dead, believing that they would be hungry in the afterlife as they had been on earth. Hades, where ancient Greeks went after death, was a place not so very different from earth. Heaven, in the minds of many people, was (and still is) an actual place where spirits acted very much as if they were still alive.

In ancient times it was believed that if one did not treat the dead according to local beliefs and customs, they would come back and do evil. That idea is also the basis for many modern ghost stories, and some vampire stories as well. Sometimes people "fed" or "bribed" their ancestors by making sacrifices to them. The Awemba tribe in Africa, for example, believed that ancestors who were not correctly treated had the power to make their descendants ill. To prevent that, living tribesmen made offerings to their ancestors—offerings of blood poured out on the ground. It isn't too hard to see how a belief in vampires could have come from that!

The gruesome Countess Bathory, that sixteenth-century Hungarian lady who butchered young girls so she could bathe in their blood, is a good example of a person who, though alive, had vampiristic tendencies because of mental or physical illness. It is even possible that some of the ghostly "undead" vampires which were seen by their victims were really alive. Suppose some poor soul, insane or with an undiagnosed nutritional disease, satisfied his craving for blood back in the early 1700s on the neck of a peasant—attacking, of course, under cover of darkest night—perhaps even cleverly letting himself into a locked house with a stolen key? That, plus superstition and terror, could explain a lot.

It is hard to tell, though, which vampires in the oldest folktales might have been of this kind. But there is little doubt about some of the more modern ones:

Fritz Haarmann, known as the "Hanover [Germany] Vampire," was a mentally ill man who killed thirty or more young boys in the early twentieth century, usually by biting them in the throat and sucking out their blood. A young girl in Brooklyn, New York, in the 1930s also had an insatiable desire to drink blood. She didn't kill anyone, but she did bite or cut one or two. The poor girl was herself convinced she was a vampire. But when

Christopher Lee, probably today's most popular living horror movie actor. Here he portrays Dracula in a British film of 1958.

she finally went to a doctor it was discovered she had a serious blood disease called pernicious anemia. Her vampirish craving for blood was merely her body's desperate attempt to make up for its own lack. The same kind of disease, or mental illness, may have been behind the stories of other modern, live "vampires"—like the man in London who was executed in 1949 for killing nine people in order to drink their blood, or the twenty-five-year-old Argentinian man who was arrested in 1960 for biting some fifteen women in the throat.

An even rarer disease, called porphyria, may well have been responsible for many a vampire tale—especially since the disease is hereditary. A person with porphyria can look pretty terrifying, for his teeth and nails take on a fluorescent glow. (Remember those Chinese and Norman vampires who were said to shine with a greenish light? Other vampires also have been said to glow green.) Porphyria victims are likely to be deformed in other ways, too, especially about the face. They are very sensitive to sunlight, so if they go out, it is usually after dark—like vampires. The disease can make them act strangely, also. Brothers and sisters in the same family often have porphyria, and the disease, though rare, is most frequent in small out-of-the-way places where many people are related to one another. Vampire stories persist in just such remote parts of the world—and frequently vampires are said to attack members of their own families, causing them to become vampires themselves. Put all these facts together and they all seem to point to porphyria's being an important explanation for vampire legends, at least in some parts of the world.

Just as disease on the part of supposed vampires contributed to these gory legends, so did disease on the part of the victims.

Take, for example, the peasants in remote mountain villages.

They would have known, of course, that blood is the source of life; everyone knew that. But they may not have known very much about disease, and perhaps there was no doctor for miles. If several people in their village fell ill, one after the other, all with similar symptoms—weakness, paleness, weight loss, even death—mightn't it have seemed to the uneducated villagers that they had been drained of blood? Mightn't they have wondered—especially if it was suggested to them—if there was a vampire on the loose? The thought that the village was in the throes of a serious epidemic might never have occurred to them.

Tuberculosis, although it is not terribly contagious, is to some extent—enough so that it was a common disease up until the middle of the nineteenth century. In its early stages it has few recognizable symptoms, and by the time symptoms appear—symptoms like weight loss and fatigue—the disease is often already far advanced. People who do not themselves come down with the disease can pass it along to others. To a person unfamiliar with the science of medicine, tuberculosis would be very hard to explain, especially when some of its more dramatic symptoms, like coughing and spitting blood, were not present. It is quite possible that many victims of vampires, especially those in rural areas, were actually victims of TB. In fact, the two were sometimes openly confused. During the 1800s in the United States, the corpses of a number of TB victims were treated as if they were vampires, either by being buried face down or by being dug up and burned when TB spread to members of their families.

There are other diseases associated with vampirism. In Danzig, Poland, in 1855 there was a severe cholera epidemic. Cholera is a frequently fatal stomach disease which has few symptoms in common with vampirism. There is one, though: people with cholera often become so dried out that their faces get extremely thin.

The Resuscitated Corpse, *an old painting, showing that the connection between cholera and vampirism was believed to be very real.*

The citizens of Danzig were so frightened of the disease that seemed to be stalking them that a vampire hysteria developed. When they began to come down with cholera, or when their fear made them sleepless and exhausted, they were convinced they were the victims of vampires.

The high rate of infant mortality in most countries before the development of modern techniques for delivering and caring for babies no doubt sparked stories of lamia-type vampires. Insect-borne diseases probably also contributed to people's belief in vampires—certainly they must have had something to do with the tiny puncture marks found in the necks of vampire victims. Insects may also have had something to do with the belief that a vampire will not attack a person who protects himself with garlic—for garlic is an effective insect repellent.

Bats, on the other hand, may have less to do with a belief in vampires than is generally supposed by those who know that Dracula sometimes took on bat shape. The blood-draining vampire bat of South America and Mexico was completely unknown to Europeans until long after their belief in vampires was well established. These bats were named after folklore vampires because they eat blood (though they lap rather than suck it). They carry disease, and if they attack the same animal—rarely humans—several times in a row, they can cause extreme weakness. Their habits no doubt contributed to the spread of vampire superstitions, especially in South America and Mexico, but it is unlikely they had much to do with originating them.

Cancer is another disease that may have been responsible for the spread of the vampire superstition. Certainly some forms of cancer have no outward symptoms except general weakness and a dramatic loss of weight; cancer can kill quickly or over a long period of time. Anemia, a blood disease which has many forms, is another obvious candidate. Again, there may be no outward signs of disease except general weakness. But the biggest candidate of all, with the possible exception of tuberculosis, is the horrible scourge that swept through Europe and much of the rest

A vampire bat. This animal was actually named after the vampire, not the other way around. However, it is such a menacing creature that it always finds its way into books about vampires.

of the world in the Middle Ages and again in the seventeenth century: plague.

Plague is spread to people from rats via fleas—but no one knew that in the Middle Ages. All people knew then was that it was a ruthless killer—25 million Europeans died of plague between 1347 and 1350, and in China in 1380, 13 million died of the same disease. Later, in 1665–1666, seventy thousand Londoners died of plague—so you can see how terrified people must

A *seventeenth-century woodcut showing what happened during the London plague of 1665. Fear of this disease, too, was so great that it gave rise to a vampire scare.*

have been of the disease and how desperately they must have searched for an explanation.

There were all kinds of theories about the cause of plague, and vampires came in for more than their share of the blame. In Scotland, for example, a Catholic man known for his evil ways died without making confession and without receiving the last rites. Plague hit his village, and his neighbors were convinced that he was the cause. He walked the streets at night, they said, tainting the air with his foul vampire's breath; people were afraid that he would attack them, sucking their blood and making them ill. After a number of people in the village had died, the man's body was dug up so it could be burned. The villagers found exactly what they had expected: an undecomposed corpse, swollen with blood and gore. They burned the body—and—so the story goes—suffered no more from plague.

Certainly such a coincidence—assuming it was one—would do much to spread the idea of vampirism, especially at a time when people lived in terror of being killed by an epidemic whose cause and nature they could not explain. It is possible, too, that there were many such coincidences, for it is likely that by the time the good people of a village got around to digging up their local "vampire" most of their neighbors had already died of plague. Those who were left were probably immune—so of course the "attacks" stopped.

Sure, you may say, fine—but how come the Scotsman's body was undecomposed when they dug him up? What of the bodies filled with warm rich blood?

What indeed? There are a number of possible explanations. Until quite recently, doctors had few surefire methods of figuring out accurately if a person who *seemed* dead really *was* dead.

Even now it is hard for doctors to establish the exact moment of death. Doctors doing heart transplants, for example, are not always sure when they can remove a donor's heart without actually killing him, even if the donor appears to be dead and certainly will be dead before long. Since it is hard to determine the exact

Drastic measures were taken to prevent spreading of the plague . . . not unlike those used to prevent the spreading of vampirism.

moment of death nowadays with modern technology, it certainly was much more difficult one or two hundred years ago. And, as a result, there were many cases of premature burial. An enterprising nineteenth-century doctor discovered many cases in one small area of France—including that of an actress who had regained consciousness while she was being embalmed. (She was so horrified to find herself being prepared for the grave that she died a few hours later.) At around the same time a French newspaper published an article about premature burial—and for the next two weeks letters poured in by the hundreds from people who said they had experienced it firsthand or knew someone who had.

There are illnesses, both physical and mental, which can bring on what is called a cataleptic condition, in which a person appears to be dead but is not. A person suffering from catalepsy may breathe so shallowly he appears not to breathe at all; his limbs become rigid, and his body grows cold as in death. He can continue in this state for a few minutes—or, in extreme cases, several years.

In the early part of this century in the United States, at least one case of premature burial occurred each week, most of them probably the result of some form of catalepsy. A young girl, for example, "died" and would have been buried promptly except for her little brother's insistence that she was still alive. The family kept the body as long as they could but finally had to take it away to be buried. Just as they were carrying the girl away, her brother thought he saw her lips move. Hopefully, he asked what she wanted—and much to everyone's amazement, received an answer: "Water."

People like the French actress and the American girl were

found to be alive before they were actually buried. But many others were not so lucky; they were really buried alive. These people died, not aboveground as their grieving relatives and friends thought, but horribly in their graves some time after they were buried. No wonder the dug-up bodies of many "vampires" were found to have moved and to have ugly, distorted expressions on their faces!

Certainly, too, the body of a person who had been buried alive would not decompose quite as fast as people would expect. It would probably take it an exceptionally long time to break down because it would never have been exposed to air after its vital functions had ceased. And what if, as surely must have happened once or twice, an unfortunate person who had been buried alive succeeded in digging out of his grave? Wouldn't he be half crazy after such an experience? Wouldn't he wander the streets, ghostlike, perhaps calling to his relatives, perhaps ready to do them injury for burying him alive? The possibilities seem almost more horrible than the vampire stories which undoubtedly sprang from such incidents!

Of course, many of the vampires dug up had been buried for years without decomposing. So was a nonvampire who was dug up from a Danish peat bog. He had lain for hundreds of years without decomposing—preserved by the sphagnum moss of the bog. Soil elsewhere, notably in parts of Greece, is so dry it tends to preserve, rather than decay, anything buried in it. Then, too, the cause of a person's death can slow down or speed up the rate of decomposition of the body. So can his profession: "A tanner will last you nine year," said the gravedigger in Shakespeare's play *Hamlet*—meaning that a man who had spent his life making leather out of hides would himself be partially embalmed by the preservatives he used. A variety of substances can "embalm" a body—even lightning, according to one source, and ashes. Nuns who died in a fire in Quebec in the early 1700s were found undecomposed—and full of blood—after twenty years had passed; they were dug up from beneath a thick layer of ashes. Freezing, of course, will also preserve a body.

But little of this was known back in the days when "real" vampires stalked the nighttime world. No wonder that, without all these logical explanations, people believed in vampires—no wonder when they were also so afraid of them—afraid to look closely, perhaps, at the bodies they dug up to destroy.

Of course they probably did look more closely at the bodies of vampires' victims. Closely enough to see those tiny toothmarks, over and over again. Somehow it's hard to believe that all those marks were caused by insects—or that they were always a product of people's superstitious imaginations. Folklorists can't always explain them satisfactorily and neither, it seems, can scientists. . . .

Can you?

SELECTED BIBLIOGRAPHY

Suddenly, within the last year, vampire books and stories have been appearing at a great rate. Up until recently, most written material on the subject was very old, very difficult to read, and very hard to find. Here is a list of some of the books and stories presently available—soon, perhaps, there will be more to choose from.

BOOKS

Aylesworth, Thomas G., *Vampires*. Reading, Mass., Addison-Wesley, 1972.

———, *Monsters from the Movies*. Philadelphia, J. B. Lippincott Company, 1972.

Coffman, Virginia, *The Vampyre of Moura*. New York, Ace Publishing Corp., 1970.

Cohen, Daniel, *A Natural History of Unnatural Things*. New York, The McCall Publishing Company, 1971.

Douglas, Drake, *Horror*. New York, The Macmillan Company, 1966. ("The Vampire")

Leach, Maria, ed., *Funk and Wagnalls Standard Dictionary of Folklore, Mythology and Legend,* vol. 2. New York, Funk and Wagnalls Company, 1949.

Ludlam, Harry, *A Biography of Dracula, The Life Story of Bram Stoker.* London, W. Foulsham and Company, Ltd., for the Fireside Press, 1962.

MacCulloch, Canon John Abbot, ed., *The Mythology of All Races.* New York, Cooper Square Publishers, Inc., 1964.

Ross, Marilyn, *Barnabas, Quentin, and the Body Snatchers.* New York, Paperback Library, 1971.

————, *Barnabas, Quentin, and the Nightmare Assassin.* New York, Paperback Library, 1970.

Stoker, Bram, *Dracula.* (This has been published by so many different companies, in both hardcover and paper editions, it would be impossible to list them all.)

SHORT STORIES AND NOVELLAS

Byron, George Gordon, "A Fragment."

Doyle, Arthur Conan, "The Sussex Vampire."

Le Fanu, Sheridan, *Carmilla.* New York, Paperback Library, 1970.

Polodori, John, *The Vampyre,* in *The Castle of Otranto* by Horace Walpole, edited by E. G. Bleiter, Gloucester, Mass., Peter Smith.

Stoker, Bram, "Dracula's Guest." (This is the chapter of *Dracula* that was dropped from the finished book.)

Wells, H. G., "The Strange Orchid."

INDEX

ABOUT THE AUTHOR

Nancy Garden, born in Boston, Massachusetts, spent her childhood in various parts of New England, and was graduated from the Columbia School of Dramatic Arts, receiving her master's degree from Columbia Teachers College. She has been an actress, stage lighting designer, teacher, and editor, but is mainly devoted to writing. Her published books for young people include two novels, WHAT HAPPENED IN MARSTON and THE LONERS, and nonfiction, including a companion book to VAMPIRES, called WEREWOLVES. Ms. Garden lived in New York City for several years, but now shares a home in the country with a friend and two golden retriever puppies, and spends most of her spare time gardening.